The Art of Balance

Creating Calm in a Chaotic World

John Farrelly

VERITAS

First published 2008 by
Veritas Publications
7/8 Lower Abbey Street, Dublin 1, Ireland
Email publications@veritas.ie

Website www.veritas.ie

10 9 8 7 6 5 4 3 2 1

ISBN 978 1 84730 065 2

Copyright © John Farrelly, 2008

A catalogue record for this book is available from the British Library.

Designed and typeset by Paula Ryan
Printed in the Republic of Ireland by Betaprint, Dublin

*Veritas books are printed on paper made from the wood pulp of managed forests. For every tree
felled, at least one tree is planted, thereby renewing natural resources.*

Contents

Introduction

In the fast-paced chaos of the modern world people are steadily detaching from the parts of their existence that they cherish most. This can manifest itself in various ways – from a feeling that 'something is missing in life' right the way through to burnout, low productivity, insomnia and stress-related illness. Many of these people are searching for a new way to live their life. This search is turning from a small trickle to a huge stream. Yet throughout their trek people continually find themselves being dragged back into living according to the expectations of others at work and at home, constantly putting the needs of others before their own, getting stuck in old ways of thinking or, worst of all, giving up trying to create a new path due to fear of change.

The way we think and therefore the way we take action is based in our deeply held assumptions and beliefs about life. We are generally not conscious of our belief system, so it influences us without our knowing. Commonly, our belief system is based in fear, because it developed as a protection mechanism. This makes control the focus of our life, to keep fear in abeyance. Beliefs create 'automatic thinking', which becomes the way we respond to everything.

This book allows us to explore our assumptions and to replace fear-based beliefs with love-based beliefs. Self-knowledge is the antidote to fear. Without belief in yourself, the world will always be a scary place. Without fear, there is freedom. Through this book, the reader will glimpse the natural inquisitiveness of childhood, learn to direct curiosity inward and become a student of self. Self-awareness leads to honesty with and respect for yourself, which will in turn lead to an unshakable belief in others.

Often, we spend our lives responding to the events of life, those things that happen around us. Rarely, however, do these represent things that matter most to us. What's far more important than life's events is the recurring pattern in those events; here we find the underlying meaning in life. No matter what is happening in your life, the view is very different when seen from a bigger perspective. *The Art of Balance* facilitates you to take a step back and begin to separate yourself from the 'stuff' of life and engage the perspective of 'What's possible?' or 'What is this trying to teach me?' instead of from the more common perspective of 'What's wrong now?' The truth of life is that underneath the chaos of daily living are both order and harmony that follow the natural rhythm and cycles of the universe.

Through a series of easy to read, enjoyable and relevant chapters readers can begin to identify balance blockers and explore practical ways to achieve balance in spite of the chaos of modern living. An array of simple exercises and activities will help balance the mind, for the key to balance is both in our head and our heart. We need to learn to think differently! So many people feel guilty about focusing on life balance, as they believe taking time out for themselves is an unproductive use of time. Contrary to the commonly held belief that taking care of self is 'selfish', it is actually the way in which we regenerate ourselves and our energy, so that we may continue to do the work we are here to do and to be the person we are here to be. Caring for yourself allows you to connect with yourself more deeply, which allows you to connect with others in a way that shares the real you, honestly and authentically. It also allows you to find a 'pace' at which you can sustain a life of meaning and purpose, a pace at which you never lose yourself.

This book will help to eliminate faulty thinking. It is amazing that we treat our cars better than we treat ourselves. What is the first thing we do when we notice our car is low on petrol? We fill our tanks! Well, living a more balanced life is about filling your tank. Those initially cynical people who reluctantly committed to living a more balanced lifestyle now report that they are more relaxed, have more time for themselves and haven't sacrificed their jobs or their families and friends in the process! In fact, once we change our thinking and learn the art of balance we attract new friends, work smarter and become more connected to the world we live in. The words in this book are all about moving from toxic to thankful, from chaos to calm and from broken to balanced.

The Need to Balance

Just as Newtonian classical physics had to give way to quantum mechanics in order to explain the growingly complex fabric of our universe, traditional models of living need to give way to more flexible, responsive and even organic ways of connecting with the world.

In the modern world calm and balance have been relegated to the back seat. We traded them in somewhere along the way for the promise of something 'out there'. We've been engaged in a desperate pursuit of what we think will bring us success and happiness in life, unaware that our desperation is leading us nowhere and that the true answer we're looking for is both inside and all around us.

This book provides insights and paths towards balance that you might follow in your own life, as an individual, a spouse, a parent or indeed in your work and community. It all starts with a new way of being.

Balance is about 'being', not about position in a hierarchy. The book examines a number of paths, specifically overcoming the past, soulful communication, spirituality, balanced relationships, raising a happy child and work–life balance. Because each one is a pursuit to be lived, not a task to be handled, you'll never be truly 'done', because there is no place to go except to be. No one path compromises another; rather each produces positive benefit for everyone.

The achievement of balance will make you both a servant and leader in life, no matter where you go or with whom you relate. There is perhaps no greater legacy to leave behind than that you have truly lived.

Outline

Chapter 1 facilitates the reader to draw a line under the past, identify mistakes and move on. Chapters 2 and 3 give the reader the opportunity to look at living from their authentic, inner source – through the human spirit and soulful communication. Those who are living their spirit are just in touch with an inner rhythm, an inner message that guides their life in a way that is simple, clear, meaningful, productive and easy, all at the same time.

If we could allow life's events and situations to teach us, instead of being a problem for us, life would get easier overnight. This is explored in Chapters 4, 5 and 6, on balanced relationships, child rearing and work–life balance. In these life pathways 'stuff' happens; what matters is how you respond. You can choose to respond by adopting a 'culture of learning' in your life. Like nature, you can choose to move only in the direction of what works. True learning asks you to change who you are at the level of being. Anything that happens in life happens in the present moment. Think about it; you can't have something happen to you in the past. With a deepening knowledge of yourself, you will be more capable of being present. And the more you live in the present, the more you will see your mind before it has impacted your choices. From this place of fresh awareness, you will make new choices, ones that are conscious. And trust in the human spirit. There is an underlying rhythm in our lives. We have the choice to both recognise it and go with its flow, by aligning our intent with the natural calm under the chaos.

Chapter 1.

Overcoming the Past

Tackling Destructive Traces

People have great difficulty understanding why destructive patterns, fights and ruptures occur in their lives and intimate love relationships. One minute they are walking happily home from work and then, before they know it, they are tearing strips off their partner or children, or fighting with a stranger in a shop queue. Very often this can be because people are interacting based on thoughts and emotions that belong to their role within their family of origin.

The first relationship we observe is that of our parents. This forms a template deep in our unconscious that affects our future choice of partner. Our parents form a model of what relationships are like and what adult males and females are about. As such, these early imprints have a profound effect on our choice of mate and our expectations with respect to a relationship.

If this early imprinting was positive, we are likely to have satisfying interpersonal relationships and a positive image of others. However, if it was negative, it may well have the opposite effect. Sometimes the effect was so negative, even though we may not be aware of it, that it can severely interfere with our interpersonal satisfaction. Repeated destructive relationships, co-dependence and generally unhealthy relationships may ensue. In these cases, professional intervention may be necessary before you can proceed towards a healthy, fulfilled life with your partner. (If in doubt, seek the help of a qualified professional trained in relationship skills.)

A good example of how traces of the past sit in our minds was given by Sigmund Freud, who cites the magic writing pad of our childhood days. We all remember 'Etch a Sketch', the toy board that you could draw on and then, as if by magic, erase the picture and begin again. As with most toys, we eventually got bored and ripped it apart to see how the magic worked. On the carbon underneath we could see traces of all the drawings – and yet we thought that we had wiped them away. The human mind works in a similar way. Traces of all the encounters and experiences we have in our life are stored in the back of our minds. Over time experiences repeat themselves and before we know it some traces are bigger and more prominent than others. These traces are the building blocks of what we call our psychological worldview. Then, in the blink of an eye, these traces take on a power of their own. They begin to shape, create and alter how we see the world. Experiences and events that fit and add to these traces we notice and are drawn to; conversely, those that do not tally with this worldview often go unseen or cause us psychological distress.

These traces, built up during childhood, are suitable for the child's world or for your role as son, daughter, brother or sister within your family of origin. However, many of these traces, evident in our behaviour, thoughts and attitudes towards our spouse and loved ones, are not useful in adult life. They can choke and suffocate a marriage or adult intimate relationship. The task for each partner is to think deeply about their behaviour and worldview; become aware of the repetitive traces and decide if they are worth maintaining or if they are a hindrance. Only the individual can decide to track and tackle their own traces. It is pointless to try to tackle your partner's traces unless you are aware of and have worked on your own.

Tense Living

Where do you choose to live? Deciding to live in a trendy leafy suburb or a rustic rural town isn't nearly as important as choosing to live in the past, present or future. Whether it's the city or country, life goes on. But can the same be said of the past or the future?

Many spend countless hours lingering in the past – past regrets, past misfortunes, past mistakes. As their thoughts remain in the past, the present quietly slips by. Lost in the past, they are unaware of the opportunities of the present. Isn't eight hours of sleep a day enough? What's the point of waking up if all we do is dream about the past or future? Instead of focusing on the tapes playing in our heads, shouldn't we open our eyes and experience the real thing?

Making the Most of the Present

The secret of life is to do our best *now*, to remain in the present. When we live by this rule, we are not guaranteed a happy past and a successful future, but at least we are doing our best now to *create* the past and future we want.

If you haven't been living by this rule, don't worry about it because the past is behind you and you are now living in a new moment of time. You are living in the moment of power. It is only in the present that we have the power to change. And when I change my actions today, I am changing tomorrow's past. As I continue to do my best each day, I build a new history of past successes, which then combines with the present to bloom into an even brighter future.

A reason people live in the past or dream of the future is to avoid present discomfort. Rather than face challenges, difficulties or pain, they seek refuge in a dream world. So, we need to develop the courage to face all challenges with a smile. It becomes easier to do so when we live one day at a time. Anyone can carry his burden, however hard, until nightfall. Anyone can do his work, however hard, for one day. Anyone can live sweetly, patiently, lovingly, purely until the sun goes down.

Making the Most of the Past

Instead of ruminating on the past, learn from it. What did you do wrong? Correct your behaviour! What did you do right? Keep doing it! Learn from the past with open eyes. Be brutally honest. Learn from what has happened, not from what you imagined has happened. Learn and move on. Use the past as a guidepost, not as a hitching post. The past should be a springboard, not a hammock. Learn to let go of the past. Until you release it, you won't be free to work on the present. And don't be afraid of the past. It can't reach out into the present and bite you. Let the dead rest in peace and focus on the only moment you are alive, which is NOW.

Pondering what might have been wastes as much time as dreaming about what might be. The twilight world of speculation is like a dense fog that obscures reality. Leave the past and re-engage with life, for what's live is so startling it leaves little time for anything else.

Making the Most of the Future

The future is pregnant with possibility, promise and potential. It is the home of hope. No matter how dire your present circumstances, no matter how desperate you may feel, no matter how severe your losses, there is always another day, a fresh beginning – tomorrow. Tomorrow brings new opportunities, but tomorrow will never come unless you persist today. So, the lesson is clear: weather the storm; survive the gale; and struggle through the tempest. In a word, persevere! Never give up!

It's Up to You

REACH UP. Stretch yourself. Don't go through life, GROW through life. Discover who you really are. Unleash the powers within you. LIVE UP to your dreams and ideals. Set goals and create meaning and purpose in your life. Remember that life is not about what you accumulate, but about what you become. Don't concern yourself with what you leave behind; rather, concentrate on what you leave within.

LIVE IT UP! Discover the grandeur of life. Soak it in. Revel in it. As the song says, 'I hope you dance'. But don't dance alone. Just as a shooting star leaves a long, brilliant trail, leave joy in your wake and share it with everyone.

WAKE UP to what is important and realise that feeling important is not that important; being important is. You can be important in the lives of others by being a source of friendship and inspiration. Most human beings are starving for understanding, acceptance and recognition. Feed their hunger by treating everyone as though they are important (which they are).

LIFT UP others with your positive spirit and encouraging words. If you want to matter, remember that everyone else does, too. So, start making a life, instead of making a living.

GROW UP. Take responsibility. Be accountable for all your actions. When you can live with their consequences, you will know what it is to be free. Don't COVER UP your mistakes. Don't shift the blame. Instead, learn from the past and move on.

Don't STIR UP trouble. Instead, be a peacemaker. Don't BLOW UP over trivial matters. Instead, be patient. Accept the inconsistencies and minor inconveniences of life.

Don't get BENT UP out of shape over the cruel remarks of others.

Instead, forgive them for their insecurity and weakness. Don't EAT UP your heart with resentment and anger. Instead, FILL UP your heart with love and understanding. Don't resent people for being people. Accept their flaws and they will likely accept yours. Don't BREAK UP friendships because of pride, lack of patience or a misunderstanding.

Don't DIG UP the dirt on others by gossiping, for when you do so, the only reputation you soil is your own. Don't THROW UP the past and hurl blame on others. Instead, CLEAN UP your act and MAKE UP with your friends and PATCH UP all your relationships, for friendships are to be cherished.

BEAR UP to the challenges life offers. FACE UP to your problems. GET UP again whenever you are knocked down. PICK UP the pieces and get on with life. We don't grow courageous by leading a life of ease. Rather, we become warriors by overcoming adversity, licking our wounds and moving forward. Should you stumble and fall, that's just a short trip on your journey, so never GIVE UP.

SUMMON UP your courage. RISE UP over your fears. Life is a glorious adventure. Embark on a quest to discover the person you can become. The rewards for overcoming our fears are great.

SPEAK UP for your rights and the rights of others, but don't SPEAK DOWN to your opponents. STAND UP for what you believe in and don't PUT UP with injustice. FIRE UP your enthusiasm and TAKE UP a cause. Contribute to life and be kind to others. You'll never regret doing so, for you'll find that you cannot become a success unless many other people want you to be.

Let those of us who are parents BRING UP our children with love. Let's not HOLD UP their progress because of criticism. Instead, in our family conversations, let's BRING UP positive subjects. And at family gatherings let's PERK UP the conversation with joyous laughter. Let's also teach our children to LOOK UP to others, giving them positive role models to aspire to.

And, like Lily Tomlin, remember that you're a somebody. Here's what she said: 'I always wondered why somebody doesn't do something about that. Then I realised I was somebody.' So, let's WRAP UP every day by reflecting on our achievements and our mistakes. Let's be grateful for our successes and learn from our missteps. Yes, life can be great, but it's all UP to you!

Getting to your Core

Each of us has our own set of values. These are what determine which aspects of life we regard as important or beneficial. Our values help determine our way of life, our entertainment, our social, political and religious interactions. Each of us holds many values and these are liable to change as we grow, reach different stages of life or have different experiences or influences in life. Some of the values we hold may be 'superficial', transitory or fitting solely the moment in which we find ourselves. Other values are more fixed and may stay with us through our life; these are our 'core values'.

Our values come from a range of sources. Our parents are a key influence on our values as we grow as children. So, too, is any church or religious background we experience. Our society, our neighbours, friends and colleagues can also have an influence on our values, as can our teachers and schooling.

Often, school can be a place of conflict, for it is there that we experience other values perhaps for the first time. Some of the values we experience in school can contradict or be in conflict with those of our parents. As we go through secondary school in particular, we start to experience values in ourselves and our peers that conflict both with our school and parents. Conflicting and unfixed values can be a major problem during adolescent and teenage years.

As we grow in years and experience, our values become more fixed, especially our set of six to ten 'core' values. It is these core values that determine what is really important to us as individuals. The surprising thing is that if you ask most people what their values are, many would not be able to give you an answer.

A good many people are leading lives unconnected with their core values. This can lead to a life of unhappiness, discontent and lack of fulfilment. Sometimes it can lead to conflict. Often the person does not know why their life seems unhappy, unfulfilled and sometimes full of conflict. Often, the cause is that the life they are living is not in accordance with their personal values.

For some people a conflict can arise within them because they are trying to live a life according to the values of a company, an organisation, or even of friends or relatives, rather than living a life according to their own core values. In doing this, the values of the other people or organisations are being met but the person's own values are being left unfulfilled.

This is not to say that a person is always wrong to seek to support and fulfil the values of other people or organisations. However, leaving your own values unfulfilled can lead to frustration and unhappiness. A key issue in this is that the person may believe they are doing the right thing by working to the values of others and yet still feel a sense of frustration and lack of fulfilment; the reason being that they may be unaware of their own values or, maybe, feel guilty of their own values where they conflict with the values of others. So, if you feel your life is unfulfilled, unhappy or maybe has too much conflict, it could be that you are leading a life that does not accord with your core values. The question is: do you know your own personal core values?

For those who want to start the discovery for themselves, try answering the following question:

What, in life, is important to you?

Don't think about your answers (yes, there's likely to be more than one thing that's important to you), at least not at first. Just write down whatever comes into your head, no matter how strange, amusing or worrying they may seem. These first answers are probably your 'gut' or 'intuitive' answers; sometimes these are closer to the truth than answers that you 'think' about. Next, think about what is important in life for you. Take some time to consider your answers before writing them down in a word or short phrase. Don't worry if some of the same answers appear in your first list; just write them down again.

Now you have two lists. Take a look at them; is there anything there that surprises you or anything that worries you? Sometimes people can be quite surprised by what they write down and occasionally they may write down something that shocks them or they feel guilty about.

Quite common words that people put on their list of values include: 'money', 'success', 'family', 'wife/husband/partner', 'growth', 'power'. If you find one, or more, of these words on your list, ask yourself another question:

What does (the word) mean for me?

So you may ask, 'What does money mean for me?' To which the answer could be: money means security, or money means success, or money means freedom, or money means being able to provide for my family. By answering the second question you can help uncover the real or underlying value for you. So for you, money is not the real value, it is 'security' or 'being successful' or 'being independent' or 'being able to provide for my family' that is the real value.

By doing these simple exercises, you are beginning to discover your personal core values. The next exercise is to ask yourself, 'How do my life, my work and my relationships help fulfil my personal values?' If you find that they do not help you fulfil your personal values then perhaps you should consider changing.

Overcoming Failure

Failure can be a beautiful experience. Why? Because it provides us with an opportunity to develop courage. Or, as Confucius said, 'Our greatest glory is not in never falling, but in rising every time we fall'. Anyone who has seen the movie *Rocky* can never forget the scene in which he continually rises after being knocked down in the ring over and over again. Bloodied and barely able to see, he continues to get up and stagger towards his opponent, while his manager shouts, 'Rocky, stay down! Stay down!'

At one time we were all just like Rocky. As infants learning to walk we would just get up after each fall. We were courageous! What happened? Why did many of us change? Well, as infants, our parents encouraged us. They brought out the courage that naturally resided in us. But as we grew and experienced the jeers instead of cheers of our peers, courage somehow got pushed into a corner of our psyche and eventually we forgot ever having it.

It's time to say: I won't take it any more; I'm going to reclaim my courage! The best way to begin is by realising that failure is an event, not a person. In other words, if you were to try something new and fail eighteen times in a row, you would not be a *failure*, but a *person* who has experienced eighteen failures. That's a big difference. So, if there's something you want to do and are unsuccessful, dust yourself off and try again! Remember, the only people who never fail are those who never try.

Success Means Never Giving Up

What did Thomas A. Edison say after 10,000 unsuccessful attempts to develop his electric light bulb? He said, 'I have not failed. I've just found 10,000 ways that won't work'. Edison realised that men do not fail; they give up trying. He realised that success means not giving up. Shouldn't we be following his example?

Failure is more than an opportunity to develop courage. It is also a valuable lesson. When we learn from our mistakes, we can avoid committing them again. Besides, to succeed in life we need experience and we gain experience by making mistakes. Don't be disheartened by failures; after all, you don't drown by falling in water; you drown by staying there.

Before a missile can hit its target, it needs feedback. Each moment it drifts from the target, the missile detects the error and adjusts its path to realign with its destination. It continues to do so until the moment of impact. Failure is also feedback. It is a reminder that we must take corrective action before we can reach our goal.

We can rejoice in our failures because each one brings us that much closer to success. The great Babe Ruth put it this way, 'Every strike out brings me closer to the next home run'. Also, here's what Thomas J. Watson, founder of IBM, had to say on the subject: 'Would you like me to give you a formula for ... success? It's quite simple, really, double your rate of failure! You're thinking of failure as the enemy of success. But it isn't at all ... you can be discouraged by failure – or you can learn from it. So go ahead and make mistakes. Make all you can. Because, remember that's where you'll find success.'

Which is better, to try something and fail or to try nothing and succeed? I think you will agree it is far better to try. Remember, there are three kinds of people: those who make it happen, those who watch it happen and those who say, 'What happened?' If we wish to belong to the first group, we have to take risks and try. So, let's start today by defying failure, learning from our mistakes and forging ahead.

Healing the Past

Research indicates that those who suffered physical, psychological, or emotional abuse as children, or were raised in households marked by violence, substance abuse, mental illness or criminal behaviour, were far more likely to develop serious illnesses as adults – everything from diabetes and bronchitis to cancer and heart disease. The good news is that our body and brain are remarkably resilient; we are fully capable of healing old wounds and reversing the damage of past adversity.

Here are ten ways to rewrite your life story:

1. **Reframe the past.** You don't have the power to change the past, but you can control how you experience it now. Instead of responding in the same habitual way when disturbing incidents come to mind, pause and take a deep breath. Then reinterpret

them. Ask yourself, 'How did that experience make me stronger? What important life lessons did it teach me?'

2. **Break the shackles of shame.** Unlike remorse or guilt, shame isn't about feeling bad for what you've done but rather for what you are. Shame is the cancer of the spirit. It makes you feel worthless and unlovable, undeserving of happiness. Always remember that shame is a lie. You are worthy of love and respect.

3. **Release the pain.** Research shows that those who write about past traumas heal faster from illnesses, visit their doctor less often and have stronger immune systems. Set aside some time and write letters to everyone who ever hurt you. No one needs to see these letters but you, so don't hold back, don't censor yourself or worry about spelling and grammar; just let out all the rage that has been festering inside, contaminating your system.

4. **Stop the slow acid-drip of regret.** The constant repetition of 'If only ...' and 'I should have ...' can destroy your health as well as your peace of mind. An important aspect of healing is to stop punishing yourself for past mistakes. Instead, forgive yourself, learn the right lessons and resolve to act differently in the future.

5. **Practice acceptance.** Nothing perpetuates the impact of old hurts more than rehashing them in your mind. It's like watching the same movie over and over again in the hope that the ending will change. Bemoaning your fate does not help you heal the past. Peace comes from accepting what was for what it was and moving on.

6. **Cultivate gratitude.** Even better than acceptance is gratitude. No matter what happened in the past, remind yourself that you have gifts to be thankful for. You may even find that you're grateful for your troubles because of what you learned from them.

7. **Create a satisfying future.** As the old saying goes, living well is the best revenge. A great way to make peace with your past is to become the person you always wanted to be. The grip of old patterns and perceptions may be so strong that you feel like a helpless victim. In fact, you are the author of your own life story and you can start a new chapter anytime you choose.

Chapter 2

Soulful Communication

Gentleness

Many of the wars around the world today tell us that there are still people who fail to realise that gentleness is more powerful than force. Words are easily spoken and quickly forgotten, but images persist. That's why the greatest teachers taught in parables, fables and stories. To help bring home the difference between gentleness and force, here is the story of *The Wind and the Sun*, written by Aesop (c 620–560 BC):

Once upon a time when everything could talk, the Wind and the Sun fell into an argument as to which was the stronger. Finally they decided to put the matter to a test; they would see which one could make a certain man, who was walking along the road, throw off his cape. The Wind tried first. He blew and he blew. The harder and colder he blew, the tighter the traveller wrapped his cape about him. The Wind finally gave up and told the Sun to try. The Sun began to smile and as it grew warmer and warmer, the traveller was comfortable once more. But the Sun shone brighter and brighter until the man grew so hot the sweat poured out of his face, he became weary and seating himself on a stone, he quickly threw his cape to the ground. You see, gentleness had accomplished what force could not.

Force is futile because it offers a temporary solution to a permanent problem. Force is met with resistance. It represses, suppresses and oppresses. Gentleness addresses the problem. It alleviates, mitigates and obviates the pain of others.

In our own lives it is appropriate to ask ourselves questions such as, How do I treat my family? Do I try to force them to comply with my wishes or does the warmth of my smile encourage them to work with me as a team? How do I handle my co-workers? Am I demanding or understanding? How do I interact with my neighbours? Am I curt and cold, or compassionate and caring? How do I treat the belongings of my friends? Do I return everything I borrowed promptly and in the same condition it was in when I received it?

When we treat others with gentleness, it shows them that we value and respect them. They may be upset and speak to us angrily, but our gentle answer may soothe their irritability and calm them down. Isn't it true that only those with faults complain about the faults of others? So, the fewer faults we have, the greater our gentleness, tolerance and compassion will be for both ourselves and others.

Gentleness is the mark of the spiritual person, one who sees the commonality of all. It is the recognition that despite our differences we are all the same. It can be easier for older people to be gentle, for their long experience has made them realise they are guilty of every fault they see in others, so how can they hold it against them? True, we will not always agree with everyone all the time, but gentleness is the understanding that we can walk hand-in-hand without seeing eye-to-eye.

Let's not wait until we are old to be gentle. Rather, today, let's join in the prayer of Alexander Pope (1688–1744): 'Teach me to feel another's woe, to hide the fault I see; that mercy I to others show, that mercy show to me.' We climb the highest peak one step at a time and we make a difference in the world one small act at a time. A gentle smile, an encouraging pat on the back, a word of praise, a friendly hand, a warm hug and a tender look are small acts, which, when added up, have a huge impact on the lives of others.

Gentleness is a way of life. It is the conduct of love. It is a balm that lessens the suffering of others. The gentle give of their time to help the sick, the elderly, the unemployed, the homeless, the needy, the mentally ill and those in prison – we should learn from their example.

Whether good or bad and whether right or wrong, our actions affect others. We set an example that helps shape their beliefs and behaviour. Like it or not, we are influencing the course of history. What type of world do we wish to have a hand in creating? One of hostility or one of harmony? One of hatred or one of honesty? The choice is ours.

Criticism

A lot of people purport the use of honesty and constructive criticism. In reality few people criticise constructively. Ask your friends or loved ones or anybody who is on the end of criticism and this is what you might learn:

> Your criticism tears down their self-esteem. They feel unloved and experience self-doubt. Before their wounds have time to heal, you sometimes stab them again and again in the same place. How can you be so cruel? How can you improve? The next time you feel like butchering someone with caustic words, pause for a moment and in your imagination realise the harm you are about to do. I'm sure you will stop.

Sometimes the harm we inflict is so subtle we are unaware of it. An example is combining praise with the word 'but'. For example, Johnny says, 'Look, mammy, I got an A in English'. His mother replies, 'That's wonderful, Johnny, BUT you have a C in maths'. The use of the word 'but' cancels the praise that preceded it. With this is mind, let's 'translate' the above conversation to see what we arrive at. Johnny: 'Look, mammy, I'm doing well at school.' Mother: 'No, you're not!'

Compare the possible outcomes of the conversation between Johnny and his mother. What would have happened if his mother had said, 'That's wonderful, Johnny. I'm going to tell Dad how clever you are. Keep up the good work'. Wouldn't that have inspired Johnny to work harder on his maths, earning more praise in the future? Instead, Johnny feels that his hard work is not appreciated because his mother said, '... BUT you have a C in maths'. Not much incentive for Johnny to try harder, is there?

What to Do when Criticised

What should you do when you are the victim of criticism? Here are some tips:

1. Use the criticism as a learning experience, i.e. **remember the pain** you feel and vow not to do the same to others.

2. **Remember they are using invisible weapons** and so they are unaware of the pain they are causing. Forgive them.

3. After being criticised, **thank them for their advice** and promise to take it into consideration. By thanking them, you are disarming their antagonism and ending the conversation peacefully.

4. **Consider the source**. The person criticising you may be

incompetent, envious or jealous. If so, after thanking them for their advice, just brush it off.

5. **Evaluate the criticism.** Although the complaint is probably not objective, there still may be some truth to what they say. Try to use this as an opportunity to grow. Remember, you are imperfect and others may see your flaws more clearly. Learn from them whenever you can, but don't return the favour by criticising others!

Criticising others is a dangerous thing, not so much because you may make mistakes about them, but because you may be revealing the truth about yourself. Also, Samuel Johnson said, 'God Himself, sir, does not propose to judge a man until his life is over. Why should you and I?' Finally, be patient with the faults of others; they have to be patient with yours.

Miscommunication

Husbands and wives separate, friends become estranged and co-workers refuse to cooperate. What causes these sad developments? More often than not, miscommunication. Good people can grow apart because of this. They thought they were communicating, but they weren't. They were talking, or sometimes 'arguing' would be more accurate. What's the difference between talking and communicating? Communicating has two parts: talking and listening. The root of the verb 'communicate' is 'to share'. How can we share thoughts and feelings unless all parties in the conversation listen with understanding as well as speak? How do we tell our spouses we love them? Not just with words, but by *listening* to what they have to say.

Often, we hear, but we don't listen. We don't absorb the points being made. What causes this breakdown in communication? It's simply because we have different backgrounds, experiences and histories. The way we view the world and interpret events differs. These differences easily lead to clashes. Once tempers rise, we say what we choose instead of choosing what we say. These quarrels amplify the misunderstanding and further the separation. True, if we share the same ideas, there would be no disagreements, but what a dull world it would be!

The first step towards eliminating miscommunication is to realise that we are all both different and the same. Because of our different backgrounds, we have different points of view. Yet we are the same in that we have a need to be understood and appreciated.

Knowledge of these simple facts is necessary to end misunderstanding. The next time you feel yourself disagreeing with someone, stop and ask yourself how their worldview differs from yours. Put yourself in their place. Try to understand where they're coming from. Always start with the assumption that, like you, they are decent people. When you think you understand (but don't necessarily agree with) their view, verify and clarify. Tell them, 'So what you are saying is … and what you mean by that is …' After going back and forth a few times, you may be surprised to learn you are in complete agreement. The moral is never rush to judgement. Don't jump to conclusions.

You may understand their point but still disagree with it. If your opinion is different, don't you want others to respect your right to disagree? Of course you do! How do you get others to respect your beliefs? By respecting theirs! Just tell them, 'I cannot say that I agree with you, but I respect your right to have a different opinion'. Often disagreements arise because we focus on the words being used instead of focusing on the speaker. Spicy, hot, cold, rich, poor, liberty and justice: although we understand these words, we interpret them differently. So focus not on the words, but the heart of the person – try to understand the person, not the words.

Occasionally, despite our best efforts, conflicts will develop. If so, there's no need to despair. After all, conflicts are always opportunities for growth. Use conflicts to learn where you went wrong and make the necessary corrections. As long as we learn from our mistakes, we will continue to move forward. When we seek to understand first and seek to be understood second, we will avoid most problems. Also, when we understand one another, there will be no need for forgiveness. If we wish to avoid misunderstanding and conflict when delivering a message, it should be stated in positive terms.

We can almost end misunderstanding if we empty our minds of biases, preconceptions, arrogance, narrow-mindedness and stereotyping. Remember, too, those we're speaking with may feel threatened. We can help to dispel such negative feelings by dispensing some kindness. Constant kindness can accomplish much. As the sun makes ice melt, kindness causes misunderstanding, mistrust and hostility to evaporate. As long as we realise that two monologues do not make a dialogue and communication does not mean others must agree with us, we should do fine. Happy communicating!

Courtesy

While driving, did you ever want to switch lanes, but were prevented from doing so by the heavy traffic? How did you feel when someone recognising your problem slowed down, waved to you and let you in? Your mounting frustration was instantly transformed into relief and thankfulness, wasn't it? Later, when you saw someone else in a similar jam, didn't you also slow down and let them in? You were sharing and spreading the kindness you received from another. How do you suppose the driver you just helped will act? Most likely, they will do likewise. Look at the power we have to sweeten the lives of others!

Sometimes, the seemingly trivial acts we perform are the most important. Courtesy is an example. We refer to it in different ways, such as civility, good manners, good behaviour, good conduct, politeness, decency, respect for others, thoughtfulness, kindness and consideration. No matter what we call it, courtesy is *not* trivial. Manners are of more importance than laws. Manners are what vex or soothe, corrupt or purify, debase or exalt, barbarise or refine us, by a constant, steady, uniform, insensible operation, like that of the air we breathe in.

Are those words too strong? Not at all. Think about it. Would a considerate person steal? Would a kind person bully? Would a thoughtful person cheat? Would a respectful person murder? No, because manners and morals flow from the same principle: consideration for others. So, as we raise the level of courtesy that is practiced in society, we lower the crime rate! We tend to think today that good manners and right morals are entirely separate. But the truth is, they are a continuum. Bad manners and high crime rates are all part of the same disease.

Unfortunately, TV, movies, the media and merchandisers often portray rudeness and aggressiveness as being 'in'. Not wanting to be left out and wishing to be 'cool', the young sometimes blindly follow the examples espoused by their heroes and heroines. Who can blame them? They don't know any better. They have yet to learn that rudeness is the imitation of strength practiced by the weak. They don't understand that polite people are enamoured with life while those who are rude are bitter.

Our manners, then, are the clothes we wear. They reveal what type of person we are. We need to teach the young by example: the strong are kind; the strong reach out and connect with others; they unite, uplift and improve the world. Those who act kindly ennoble life because they imitate God.

How are we to practice courtesy? There are as many ways as there are moments in a day. Every encounter is an opportunity. Here are some examples:

1. Whenever someone treats you kindly, show your appreciation, express your gratitude and offer your thanks. For as Seneca taught, 'There is as much greatness of mind in acknowledging a good turn, as in doing it'.

2. Recognise the achievements of others, not with shallow flattery but with sincere and warm praise.

3. Here is some good advice in the form of a Persian proverb: 'Treat your superior as a father, your equal as a brother and your inferior as a son.'

4. Be a good friend. Express your good manners with your emotions. When your friends arrive, say, 'At last!' And when they leave, say, 'So soon?' When you treat your friends kindly, you will be greatly rewarded. St Basil (329–379) explains how, 'He who sows courtesy reaps friendship and he who plants kindness gathers love'.

5. Treat others with respect. Treating royalty, political leaders or movie stars with respect is a common occurrence, but treating beggars, the homeless and ex-prisoners with respect is the mark

of greatness. It is not only the downtrodden that need respect, it is our children, too. If we don't already respect them for what they are, how can we help them become more than they are?

6. Act kindly towards others without expecting anything in return. To act in the expectation of a reward cancels out the kindness.

7. Instruct your children, for as R. Buckminster Fuller (1895–1983) wrote, 'Parents are usually more careful to bestow knowledge on their children rather than virtue, the art of speaking well rather than doing well; but their manners should be of the greatest concern'.

8. Respond to rudeness with kindness, for what better test of good manners is there than politely putting up with bad ones? We become kind by being kind and when every act we do is a kind one, the world will rejoice.

9. Be gentle in your dealings with others. As somebody once wrote, 'To find out what others are feeling, don't prod or poke. If you want to play with a turtle, you can't get it to come out of its shell by prodding and poking it with a stick, you might kill it. Be gentle, not harsh, hard or forceful'.

10. Cherish your family and reinforce it with courtesy. Oddly enough, we often treat strangers more politely than we do members of our own family. This has to stop. We need to implement a policy of 'courtesy begins at home'.

11. Never underestimate the power of your small acts of kindness. They are the pebbles that form a solid foundation for our civilisation. Without them, society would collapse.

A brief reflection on the world situation clearly reveals that our potential for evil is unlimited. Despite all our frailties, however, we are kind most of the time. That's what makes humanity so great. But there remains considerable room for improvement and the responsibility is ours. Instead of striving to be important, which is nice, let's strive to be nice, which is more important.

Gratitude

Have you ever noticed how much we begin to appreciate things and people only when there is a possibility we might lose them? In most forms of addiction therapy if the client learns to have gratitude for the small things in life, the addiction can usually be beaten. Gratitude is a powerful weapon! When gratitude is the lens through which we view the world, hassles and stress recede and our true nature of happiness shines through. There is evidence for this: research suggests that grateful people have more energy and optimism, are less bothered by life's hassles, are more resilient in the face of stress, have better health and suffer less depression than the rest of us. People who practise gratitude – and yes, it is something one can learn and improve – are also more compassionate, more likely to help others, less materialistic and more satisfied with life.

In a psychological experiment around gratitude and thankfulness hundreds of people were divided into three groups, each of which was instructed to keep a different type of journal. One group recorded daily events, another recorded hassles and another made lists of what they were grateful for. This last group reported more alertness and optimism and better progress towards goals. These people also felt more loved. As my mother used to say, you catch more bees with honey than with vinegar, and when you are appreciative and kind, other people mirror that back.

If people were to make gratitude a daily practice, fear and hatred might finally be overcome by love and compassion. But even if we can't change the world, we can always change ourselves. With that in mind, several years ago I decided to make gratitude and appreciation part of my daily spiritual practice. I had found myself taking life for granted and complaining when little things weren't to my liking. Because gratitude is a great antidote to whining and nit-picking, I decided to adopt an easy exercise from Benedictine practices. The idea is that gratefulness cultivates mindfulness, the ability to be present in life with the open-heartedness of a child. He suggests that before bed, you give thanks for one thing for which you've never before thought of being grateful.

When you practice gratitude, you naturally search for kindness, love and goodness throughout the day so that you'll have something new in mind to be grateful for when bedtime rolls around.

'People who practice gratitude are more compassionate, less materialistic and more satisfied with life.'

Gratitude Tips

- **Teach your kids:** if you have children, giving thanks before bedtime can be a delightful ritual that helps develop a healthy and loving attitude towards life.

- **Appreciate people:** make it an everyday practice. Tell them what a good job they do, how kind they are or how nice they look, as long as it's absolutely true!

- **Put it in a letter:** write to a person who made a difference in your life this year. Be specific about how and why their action enriched your life.

Judging

What a joy when you buy something, take it home and the label effortlessly peels off leaving not a trace of gummy guck behind. However, when the opposite happens and it stubbornly adheres to your new item, whether it's a gift or a goody for yourself, it's horrible. Not only is it frustrating to spend time trying to remove it, but what is new begins to look used and old. The half-peeled paper cheapens the product regardless of how valuable it is. Somehow it seems devalued.

The same thing happens when we label others and ourselves. Another word for it is 'judgement'. And when, like a dodgy label, we affix the judgment with super glue – what a mess. For most of human history people have stood in judgment of each other. We often hear the phrase 'constructive criticism' or 'the truth should be told'. But the bottom line is the judging say more about the judge than the judged.

How we treat others is simply a reflection of how we feel about ourselves. When we value ourselves, we cannot devalue another. Secure people do not put other people down. They accept others as they are and look for their positive qualities. That does not mean smiling on a bad situation or tolerating harmful behaviour in another. It means intuitively understanding people and situations and knowing when, and when not, to act or speak. There is a vast difference between judgement and intuition. Intuition allows you to discern the truth about an individual or situation. It works to protect you and helps you to make healthy decisions. Judgement, on the other hand, is a critical assessment stemming from fear. It's cold, calculated and limiting.

Intuition presents you with insights that lead to actions that are thoughtful and loving, no matter how tough they appear to be.

Intuition is a response, not a reaction. Intuition is healing, not harmful. It arises from the voice within that can only be heard when there is no judgement taking place.

You will never have enough information about people to judge them accurately – so why bother? The path of judgement leads nowhere. It is a trap that enslaves the person making the judgment. The next time you are about to cast a quick judgement, ask yourself the following questions: Is it true? Is it useful? Is it necessary?

It can be very difficult to refrain from making snap judgements about others, especially when everybody else is doing it, but you are responsible for your own evolution, not others. Do you want to meander aimlessly with the herd or would you like to rise above it to where you can see clearly and chart your own course?

The key to removing labels is to begin by valuing yourself. Your sense of true value cannot be understood at the level of the intellect. It needs to be acknowledged and understood at the level of feelings. It is heartfelt. Ponder on the miracles of the universe: the glorious galaxies; the sun, moon and stars; the exquisite designs, sounds, colours and fragrances of nature; the eclectic and creative array of animals; a newborn baby. Awaken to the beauty of life. As part of this how can you be any less than miraculous?

That very truth, when deeply felt, will prevent you from devaluing yourself or others. People you might have walked away from in the past because of hasty judgements might even become wonderful new friends. And never again will you be intimidated or influenced by the judgements of others. What people think of you will become none of your business. You will be too busy designing the life you truly want.

Controlling Anger

Anger broadcasts our own weakness. When we vent our anger, we are effectively shouting, 'I'm scared! I'm frustrated! I'm hurt!' That's another way of saying, 'I'm weak!' After all, we are only as big as the things that make us angry.

Examples of frustration include becoming angry when someone takes too long at the ATM machine, cuts you off in traffic or carelessly bumps into you. However, like it or not, people will always do these things. We have no control over the behaviour of others. To become angry because the world doesn't behave as we would like it to is childish, even infantile. When people act as I described above, they are not being mean; they are just being people. When we understand this, we can remain calm and peaceful.

When others do not follow our wishes or seemingly disrespect us, we become angry because of fear. We are afraid that we can no longer control them. But it was never intended for us to control others. Guide others by our example? Yes. Control others by power? No. Our desire for control is not wrong; it is just misdirected. It is ourselves that we need to control. When we give up our wish to control others and our environment, we will find that we have little to be angry about.

People say and do stupid things. They can hurt us. And when they do, the temptation is to get angry. But we don't have to. We can forgive them! It's not so hard to forgive others when you remember we are all the same. Nobody is perfect; we all have faults. How can we get angry with people for behaving like people? Besides, every time you give someone a piece of your mind, you make your head a little emptier!

Despite good reasons for not getting angry, it's a difficult habit to break. That is because it is often more comfortable to feel angry than to feel the underlying fear, frustration or pain. Here's an important point to consider: the consequences of one's anger are often far worse than that which caused it. As a simple example, in a heated moment you may blurt out something you later wish you had not said, but the harm is already done. You cannot take back the past. The moral? Don't get angry!

Not that all anger is bad. On the contrary, anger can be justifiable and may be necessary. As Henry Ward Beecher wrote in 1887, 'A man that does not know how to be angry does not know how to be good'. Outrage over injustice is a good example. Angry American and South African people brought about sweeping political reform and civil rights, strengthening their countries. Another example: if we have to fight to protect our family or flee from a threat, anger will provide us with the strength to act.

Nevertheless, more often than not, anger is harmful and can result in the following problems:

- Alienation of others: you feel nobody likes you and you are right! Nobody likes an angry person. How can you get your message across by getting cross?

- Health problems: according to a study of more than 1,000 people at a Western Electric factory in Chicago, over a twenty-five-year-period, those with anger-management problems were at a high risk of dying from coronary problems, as well as cancer. Chronic anger is also linked with weakening the immune system, leading to life-threatening illnesses.

- When not managed, anger can lead to rage, hate and violence.

- If not carefully monitored, anger becomes chronic and can spiral out of control.

Tips on Anger Management

- Anger will never disappear so long as thoughts of resentment are cherished in the mind. Anger will disappear just as soon as thoughts of resentment are forgotten.

- The greatest remedy for anger is delay. Counting back from fifty not only provides a delay, but shifts brain activity from the emotional part to the analytical part of the brain, decreasing the intensity of the unwanted emotion.

- Study relaxation and meditation techniques to reduce stress.

- Discuss the situation, not the person; discuss the unwanted behaviour without name-calling.

- Remaining calm allows you to examine the options and seek solutions. Getting angry blocks clear thinking.

- No one can make you angry: whether you become angry or not depends on how you choose to react to circumstances.

Chapter 3

Spirituality and Well-being

A Grateful Heart

How can one awaken to a different way of being? One way to do so is to remember all the suffering we have avoided and learn to live with a grateful heart. Think about it! Are you in desperate need of an organ transplant? Have you lost the use of your limbs? Have you lost your sight or hearing? Do you suffer from a mental illness? Are you locked behind prison bars? Do you have a serious illness, such as cancer, epilepsy or Parkinson's disease? If you have answered 'No' to these questions, you are rich. What good is all the wealth in the world to those who have lost their health or freedom? And to those who have answered 'Yes' to one of the above questions, are there others who are far worse off than you? Are you rich compared to them?

Another way to awaken is to remember all the blessings you have. Do you have a family and friends? Do you have a job and a place to stay? Do you have sufficient food to eat or enough clothes to wear? Do you have time to relax and enjoy yourself? Do you have libraries, parks, schools and community centres in your neighbourhood? How rich you are compared to the lonely, the unemployed and the homeless.

The doorway to abundance, then, is a grateful heart. The windows are our attitude and ability to see the possibilities. Much good can be done with wealth and possessions, but care of the spirit comes first, for what good are riches to unhappy people? Muhammad (570–632) expressed it this way: 'Riches are not from abundance of worldly goods, but from a contented mind.'

Are you rich or poor? Well, the terms are relative. There is always someone richer or poorer than you are. So, you are what you think you are for poverty consists in feeling poor. If you experience joy, fun, pleasure, exuberance, enthusiasm, discovery, understanding, hope, laughter, wonder and love, who can deny that you are rich? True riches well up from the soul and flow into our lives. Beware of negative thoughts and beliefs for they are what clog our spiritual 'blood vessels'. Nurture positive thoughts and allow abundance to freely flow.

We can focus on only one thing at a time. So, if we focus on our blessings, we will not be engaged in thoughts of poverty, scarcity or lack. Besides, gratitude attracts abundance, for when we are aware of its presence we are quick to discover new opportunities that come our way. Thankfulness also benefits our relationships. After all, people delight in giving to those who appreciate it and stop giving to those who are unappreciative.

An interesting irony of life is we find what we seek by giving it away. How do we make friends? Isn't it by first becoming one? How do we win respect? By first respecting others. The same principle applies to a grateful heart. The more we try to give it away, the more it multiplies and comes back to us. Be kind. Be generous. Be helpful. And when you are, you will discover you live in an immensely kind, generous and helpful world.

If the path you're treading seems a bit rough, courage is the steamroller that will smooth the way for you. A grateful heart, then, is not about the stuff we collect, but about awakening to the riches in our midst and the riches in our minds, hearts and souls.

Grace

Grace is the exercise of love, kindness and mercy to benefit or serve another. Other terms we could use include goodwill, compassion, benevolence, charity and brotherly love.

We are social beings, dependent on one another. Our birth, education and personality would not have been possible without the cooperation of others. Drawing upon our spiritual heritage, whatever it may be, allows us to use grace as a social lubricant. It eliminates friction and allows us to work together harmoniously. So, its role is critical. We either live with grace or allow civilisation to fall apart and live in disgrace.

Some describe grace as the kindness we offer those who are undeserving of it. But there are none who are undeserving. Are there any among the birds of the air or fish of the sea that are undeserving of life? Neither are there any among the men, women and children who populate the earth. Everyone needs kindness. Don't the rich as well as the poor grow hungry? Don't the strong as well as the weak grow thirsty? Who is there that does not struggle and has no need for kindness? As for those who are unkind, they need it the most. Hasn't the grace that we are imbued with been given to us to nurse the wounds of others?

In living a life of grace, our goal is first to do good, second to do good often and third to do nothing but good. It is in aiming for the third goal that we will strike the second. The advantage of doing good is it awakens us to the countless good deeds of others and the beauty of life. Whereas, if we stray from the path of goodness, our vision grows dim, until all we see is cruelty and we become cynical.

The Path of Grace is neither to the right nor to the left. It is neither liberal nor conservative. It favours neither the warmongers nor the appeasers. Rather, it is a middle path. It is the Path of Healing, for grace is the balm that heals the wounded heart. The Path of Grace is the Path of Bringing-together; the Path of Win-Win; the Path of Mutual Respect; the Path of Understanding, Tolerance and Love. It is the Way of Peace and therefore is a path we should embrace.

Don't let illness and other forms of misfortune distract you from leading a life of grace, which includes bearing your suffering with a smile. After all, if you cannot accept your own pain, how will you be able to help others accept theirs? And don't be discouraged by your imperfections because we learn how to be good by conquering our own faults. Besides, what merit is there in doing good, if it doesn't require any effort on our part? So, stretch yourself. Most of us do not realise how enormous our potential is. If we are unaware of the wrongdoing we are capable of, how can we be aware of the good we are capable of? Be patient with your progress. For, as Thomas Adams taught in the mid-seventeenth century, 'Grace comes into the soul as the morning sun into the world; first a dawning; then a light; and at last the sun in his full and excellent brightness'.

Any inspirational stories, motivating quotations or heart-warming anecdotes that we may relate will soon be forgotten, but our acts of kindness will linger indefinitely in the minds and hearts of those we help. So don't bother saving money for flowers and a monument for your grave; instead, leave behind an endless trail of good deeds. We must never underestimate our importance, for people do not learn about grace from books and institutions, but from other people, from role models. Our actions will either draw others closer to or further from goodness. Let's not take our responsibility lightly.

How do we become full of grace? By dispensing it! We fill our cup by emptying it. All we have to do is become the kind of person we would like to be with. As we carry out our acts of grace, let's remember that the kindness planned for tomorrow doesn't count for today. Also, take no thought of the thought of others. For it is better to do good and be considered nasty than to be nasty and considered good.

Silence

We all have within us a centre of stillness surrounded by silence. Yet, for some, silence and stillness are elusive. Caught up in the hustle and bustle of daily life, they find it difficult to drown out the clamour swirling about them. Even if they can retreat to a quiet spot, there is still the endless chatter in their minds to deal with. By chatter, I mean the swarm of thoughts that endlessly races through our minds. This incessant self-talk is like ripples on the surface of a pool, obscuring the stillness and serenity that lies deep within.

Stress can be a friend, for when it arrives, it gently tells us: 'You need a break. You need to find solace in solitude. Dive deeply into the silence within, for it is in silence that we rejuvenate.' Once we develop the habit of regularly visiting our inner oasis of silence, we will discover that there isn't any noise after all, just the sounds of life.

Some find their inner stillness through the path of meditation. Yet, it isn't necessary to sit quietly with eyes closed to experience the tranquillity of silence. It is just as accessible when enjoying nature or taking a walk. Lao-Tzu (c. sixth century BC) stated: 'Just remain in the centre, watching. And then forget that you are there.' In other words, we first become absorbed *by* what we see, then become absorbed *in* what we see. For example, we may see a dewdrop resting on a flower petal. At first we see its sparkling beauty and are later overcome by the power of its silence. Finally, it and its surroundings absorb us until nothing remains but silence.

So, meditation – helpful as it is – isn't necessary to discover the sanctuary of silence. A simple walk will do. In fact, even that is unnecessary, you do not need to leave your room. Remain sitting at your table and listen. Do not even listen – just wait. Do not even wait – be quite still and solitary. The world will freely offer itself to you to be unmasked; it has no choice. It will roll in ecstasy at your feet. To discover silence is like an orphan discovering their parents, for silence – nothingness – is the womb from which all that is has come forth. Therefore, when you search for nothing(ness), you find everything.

Silence is the great revelation. We may turn to books for revelation, but the authors of the books we read found the interlude of silence to be a source of inspiration and an opportunity to fashion their thoughts. So, by entering our own inner silence, we can bypass authors and go direct to the source, for silence is as full of potential wisdom and wit as the unshorn marble of a great sculpture.

There are some that busy themselves in all manner of rituals and practices to prepare themselves for another life. But as they chase after a future paradise, they kick up clouds of dust that hide the grandeur of this life. Instead of placing our hopes in a future life, why not make the most of what we already have? Stepping into the pool of silence helps us to experience joy now.

Perhaps you have seen a ray of sunshine pierce a black sky and give birth to a rainbow. When faced with staggering beauty, what do you say? Usually nothing! You are rendered speechless. To gasp in amazement at the incomprehensibility of the universe is to taste the waters of silence. Awe, wonder and joy are silent. They beckon you, but their call is silent. To be aware of their presence we have to be still and listen.

Silence can very often be the answer to our questions, for true silence is not the absence of noise, but the presence of the Divine.

Silence is the cave through which the soul must travel, clearing out the dissonance of life as we go, so that the God who is waiting there for us to notice can fill us.

If you wish to experience life rather than be swept away by it, be sure to set aside some time each day, no matter how brief, to wade in the pool of silence. For there you will be able to recharge your batteries, tap into your inner wisdom, experience the gifts of wonder and awe, and join hands with all that is.

Faith

'It can't be done. It's physically impossible for a human being. One would fall unconscious before it could be done.' These were some of the comments of renowned athletes, coaches, psychologists and physicians, who were discussing the possibility of running a mile under four minutes. They believed it was impossible. And as long as they held that belief, it was. Then along came Roger Bannister, a British medical student who lived by faith instead of belief. What's the difference? Belief is what others tell you; faith is what your inner voice tells you.

Unencumbered by negative beliefs and brimming with faith in himself, Roger Bannister shocked the sports world on 6 May 1954 by running the mile in 3:59.4. Suddenly, 'the impossible' proved possible and the shattering of the old belief was heard around the world. Bannister's feat was all the more amazing when you consider the following facts.

1. As a busy medical student, the only time he had to practise was during his lunch hour; he practised every day for forty-five minutes and spent fifteen minutes for lunch.

2. Although the track where he broke the record was supposed to be level, it had a slight upward slope, making the race even more gruelling.

3. The race took place on a windy day.

Bannister's victory destroyed the artificial barrier that prevented others from running the mile under four minutes. After everyone realised it was now possible, it only took forty-six days before the record was broken again by Australian athlete John Landy. Today, of course, 'the impossible' has become a common occurrence. In fact, New Zealander, John Walker, has already smashed the four-minute barrier one hundred times! And Morocco's Hicham El Guerrouj has shaved the time to 3:43:13!

'He must be mad! Imagine! Mr Edison is trying to create light in his laboratory despite two fundamental laws of physics that make it impossible. First, there can be no light without combustion. Second, there can be no combustion in a vacuum.' The experts at the time may have known about physics, but they didn't understand the human spirit. The incandescent lamp was already burning brightly in the mind and heart of Edison. Because of his faith, he persisted, until one day his faith unlocked the secret and achieved 'the impossible'.

The message is clear. Faith is like a key that unlocks our potential. It knows no doubt, hears no discouragement and sees no insurmountable barriers. It is resolute. With faith everything is possible. That's why Christ said, 'According to your faith let it be done to you' (Matthew 9:29). Why aren't there more Roger Bannisters in the world? Is it due to a lack of faith? No, there is no such thing as a lack of faith. We all have plenty of faith; it's just that we have faith in the wrong things. We have faith in what can't be done rather than what can be done. We have faith in lack rather than abundance. There is no lack of faith. Faith is a law.

Faith is the realisation that we can accomplish whatever we set out to do, as long as we work at it. People of faith realise the universe is here to support us, so they surrender to their dreams and leap into the unfamiliar without fear. When you get to the end of all the light you know and it's time to step into the darkness of the unknown, faith is knowing that one of two things will happen: either you will be given something solid to stand on, or you will be taught how to fly.

When Henry Ford was asked if he ever worried, he answered, 'No, I believe God is managing affairs and that He doesn't need any advice from me. With God in charge, I believe everything will work out for the best in the end. So what is there to worry about?' Faith in life, such as Mr Ford's, helps us to eliminate anxiety and reach our potential. No wonder someone wrote, 'He who loses money, loses much. He who loses a friend, loses more. But he who loses faith, loses all'.

Every great endeavour flows from faith. It is only after we place our trust in our dream that we can begin to materialise it. Faith is not fanciful; it is logical, for it is based on understanding the laws of life. All that we have seen teaches us to trust the Creator for all we have not seen. Faith is not belief without proof, but trust without reservation. Perhaps our faith cannot move mountains, but what's to stop us from climbing them? Let's cling to our faith, for it is the dawn of a new tomorrow.

Take Heart

All objects, however large or small, have an essence (nature) and act (do things). If objects did not act, there would be nothing to distinguish them from nonexistent objects. The essence of the sun, for instance, is that of a nuclear furnace and among its actions, it sends a stream of photons to the earth that nourishes plant life, which in turn produces oxygen and makes other forms of life possible. Magically, the photons not only help create life, but make it possible for life to see itself. That is, we can see thanks to the photons that strike our retinas.

It is by observing and experiencing nature that we come to understand the essence and actions of things. What is the essence of man? It is happiness. And happiness is existence aware of itself. What is the natural action of man? It is love. As infants, we are overflowing with happiness, taking delight in ourselves and the world. We express that happiness by embracing our inner and outer worlds with love. We radiate endless streams of love. We are all born for love. It is the principle of existence and its only end.

Since love is all we knew, it is all we expected. But something odd happened. Born to love; we learned to fear. We fear that our love will not be returned unless certain conditions are met. It is no longer okay to be ourselves, but we must become what others want us to be. For example, if I'm uncomfortable and cry at 4 a.m., I may upset mammy and daddy. If my room is untidy or I 'pester' my parents with pleas to play, I may be met with cold reproaches instead of warm hugs or stern rebukes instead of gentle pats on the head. The music of laughter may fade into the noise of anger and silence. The world around me changes from one of beauty to one of fear. Each step I take places me in danger of upsetting someone.

Is it surprising that we grow stressful, fearful and resentful and our love shuts down? We need to find our way back to our original heart. Once we mature, understand our true nature and what led to our problems, we can decide to change and open our hearts to love. It's simple. Go ahead and do what you want to do, i.e., love the world. The only thing that stops you now is the fear of being hurt. But you cannot be hurt if you expect nothing in return. Life is unconditionally wonderful, so love it unconditionally.

Love your family, your job, your country and everyone you meet without any strings attached. Love all that has been created by God, both the whole and every grain of sand. Love every leaf and every ray of light. Love the beasts and the birds, love the plants, love every separate fragment. If you love each fragment, you will understand the mystery of the whole resting in God. Leo Tolstoy, wrote, 'Love is life. All, everything that I understand, I understand only because I love. Everything is, everything exists, only because I love. Everything is united by it alone. Love is God and to die means that I, a particle of love, shall return to the general and eternal source'. Buddha's simple message was, 'Love the whole world as a mother loves her only child'.

For centuries, mystics have sought to experience God by depriving their bodies of food, sleep and comfort and by spending countless hours in contemplation or deep meditation. They were successful in their quests, but it isn't necessary to go to such extremes. All we need do to experience God is to experience God's work, which is unconditional love. When we open our heart to love, we open our heart to God. When we experience unconditional love, we experience God.

What better way to create balance than by accepting all those we meet without conditions. We can allow them to be themselves. Every encounter, no matter how brief, is an opportunity to nurture, be nurtured, or both. When we love others unconditionally, we shower them with understanding, encouragement and forgiveness whenever necessary. Some of those you love will return love. They will love you, not for what you are, but for what they are when they are in your presence. You will both experience love for the future good you bring out in each other.

Love is what we are born with. Fear is what we learn. The spiritual journey is the unlearning of fear and prejudices and the acceptance of love back in our hearts. Love is the essential reality and our purpose on earth. To be consciously aware of it, to experience love in ourselves and others, is the meaning of life. Meaning does not lie in things. Meaning lies in us.

Love

Although we may hesitate before arriving at the one most important thing in life, it is an easy matter to think of several things that are important to us. Some of the things that immediately come to mind are a job, money, friends, food and shelter, and a spouse and family. Now, we cannot get any of the above without the help of others. So, how do we get their help?

Life gives back to us what we give to it. So, if I help others, what do you suppose they will do? That's right, they will help me. Because we need the help of others to reach our goals, one of the most important things in life is to help others, thereby receiving their help. But don't misunderstand: the purpose of helping others is not because we need their help, but because they need our help.

How do you feel when you are served by an ingratiating waiter in a restaurant? It is not pleasant when a waiter fawns on you because he wants a big tip. But when the waiter is sincere and offers impeccable service because he takes his job seriously, it is a delightful experience. For this simple reason, when we help others, sincerity and the desire to always do and be our best must be our guiding principles.

But what causes us to serve others with a pure motive? Isn't it love? Now we can answer the question. The most important thing in life is love because love is our soul purpose. Now that we know the answer, we can begin to reflect on the meaning of love and the fruit it bears.

Love means to cherish, hold dear and treasure. We do not hurt, harm or cause pain to those we love; rather, we seek to relieve their suffering. Also, love is liberating because it is the absence of fear. It frees us from suspicion, hostility, envy and resentment. It rejoices in the achievements of others. It is not about wanting people; it's about wanting people to be happy. It's not about wanting to possess or control others; it's about wanting to set them free.

Here is an excellent description of love by William Arthur Dunkerley, 1852–1941: 'Love ever gives. Forgives, outlives. And ever stands with open hands. And while it lives, it gives. For this is love's prerogatives – to give and give and give.' Love is all there is. What more do we need to know?

Before we can love others, we have to discover and experience it for ourselves. Although it is helpful to say we first need to love ourselves, it is also inaccurate to say so. You see, to love oneself implies two people: the lover and the beloved. But we are not two; we are one. So, it is more accurate to say that when we become still and plunge into our depths, we will discover that we are love. Love is our very nature. This becomes clear when we watch infants smile at strangers. Is it not by love alone that we succeed in penetrating to the very essence of being?

Love is not about feeling good; it is about doing good. A perfect example of love in action is Mother Teresa. But how did such a physically tiny woman, barely five feet tall, find the energy to work so tirelessly? The answer can be found in the fact that love feels no burden, thinks nothing of trouble, attempts what is above its strength. It is therefore able to undertake all things and it completes many things.

When we do all things with love, we infuse our tasks and ourselves with energy. Nevertheless, after considering the extraordinary hurdles overcome by Mother Teresa, we may feel painfully inadequate and doubt that we can make much of a difference. At such a time, we should earnestly listen to her own words: 'Do not think that love in order to be genuine has to be extraordinary. What we need is to love without getting tired. Be faithful in small things because it is in them that your strength lies.'

Mother Teresa also exemplified one of the fruits of love, which is respect for others. When asked by a reporter if she tried to convert those she helped, she replied, 'Of course I convert. I convert you to be a better Hindu or a better Muslim or a better Protestant. Once you've found God, it's up to you to decide how to worship him.' It would bode well for us to follow her example, for if we cannot respect others, we cannot respect God.

Innately, we seek freedom, joy and endless growth. They are the ingredients for happiness and they are also the fruit of love. No longer a hostage of anger, a captive of greed or a prisoner of negative thinking, we are freed by love to be ourselves. As to joy, it is the natural by-product of bringing joy to others. And for endless growth to flourish, we need an environment of love, for we cannot learn from those we don't love. Love allows us to accept others and makes us willing to listen to what they have to say, the reward of which is knowledge, learning and growth.

The essence of love is kindness, Those who are portals of love are kind, gentle and humble. They express their love by serving others and their service provides meaning and purpose in their lives. On the physical plane, an enlarged heart is a malady, but spiritually, an enlarged heart embraces more and more of humanity, raising our consciousness. As our heart expands, we come to love everything under the sun: the streams, brooks, trees and creatures of the forest. Love is all we have, the only way that each can help the other. When we immerse ourselves in love, we get a taste of eternity, for brief is life but love is eternal.

Presence

Every day, we open our eyes, get out of bed, eat breakfast, brush our teeth, talk to our families and rush to do our work. And most of the time, our minds are somewhere else. When we get out of bed, we are thinking about something we should have done yesterday; when we talk to our children, we are thinking about the phone call we need to make; when we walk around the supermarket, we are thinking about the chocolate we shouldn't have eaten – or want to eat or are going to eat. Or how great our lives are going to be when we lose weight or get a promotion or fall in love.

We often spend our lives, each day, in every moment, thinking about what we already did or are going to do and we completely miss what we are doing. It's like eating a fabulous meal while talking on the phone and watching TV. The meal ends and you haven't tasted a thing because your attention was elsewhere.

This lack of attention leads to a tremendous spiritual hunger that we can't quite name. We get fooled into thinking that it's about something we don't have yet, when it's really something that is unfolding minute by minute, right in front of our eyes. We keep believing that if we go after the next big thing – the job, the car, the house, the perfect dress – the hunger will be filled. And yet over and over we find that filling the hunger isn't about acquiring more things; it's about noticing what we already have and already are.

When I talk about presence, clients give me suspicious stares. Some decide that they don't like me and want their money back. Presence sounds stupid. 'C'mon, John. You make it sound so simple. What about my crappy relationship, or the fact that I have three kids under the age of five and not one second for myself the entire day? How can I be present in my life as it is, if that life makes me unhappy?' Good question, I say. And it is.

So, in the beginning, practising presence needs to stay very simple. You start by feeling alive in your arms and legs. The reason that living in your body is quite helpful is because the alternative – living in your mind – can drive you insane. There is no particular pattern to your thoughts; in a split second, they zing crazily from the time you fell from your swing when you were six to what you are going to say to the person who insulted you yesterday.

If you try to follow your thoughts, you get lost in fantasies, resentments and anticipated disappointments. There is no ground, nothing solid to hold on to, no way of bringing yourself back to what you are doing now, this very second. You get to the end of a day – or the end of your life – and you wonder where you've been. (And the answer is: lost in thought!)

In the morning, before you get out of bed, focus your attention on your right foot, feeling your toes, your ankles, the back of your foot, the arch of your foot. Then begin sensing your calf, your shin, your knees. Continue moving all the way up through your right hip and then focus on your right hand, fingers, wrist and elbow. When you get to the shoulder, move across to your left shoulder and down this arm to your hand; then go from the left hip to the left foot. This should take about five minutes.

During the day, every time you remember, sense your arms and legs again, just for a few seconds. This will help you land in your body and bring your mind back to the present moment; it will give you a kind of mountain-solid feeling.

When you are present, nothing is missing. Time seems to stretch. And the reason it does is because it's our thoughts – our crowded, worried minds – that make us feel so rushed. When you are present, a day seems like a week; a month, like a year. Presence enables you to see that this body, your home, the place you've spent years trying to change, is actually a satisfying place to be.

Chapter 4

Balanced Relationships

Love Matters

Giving and receiving are the basic ingredients for most relationships, but it is a rare relationship that is based more on intentions of giving instead of receiving. 'What have you done for me lately?' seems to be the question everyone is asking their boyfriend, wife or significant other these days. Maybe a better question to ask would be, 'What have I done to deserve something good in return?' In our efforts to find and maintain loving relationships, many of us behave as if we are bargain hunting. 'How can I get more for less?'

Love is a noun in the dictionary. Loving is a verb – an action word. The act of loving someone is something that has to be done, not just said. One mistake many people make is paying too much attention to mainstream media and its collective definition of love. The popular talk shows and shock shows are hosted by people who understand and capitalise on knowing what the public wants to see and hear, packaging exactly that and delivering it. It's about their bottom line.

We would all do well to re-examine and re-define our definition of love from time to time. Ask yourself if you could be a more loving man or woman. Like the old saying goes, 'you get more bees with honey than with vinegar'. A lack of forgiveness gets in the way of the positive flow of love. Did you ever notice how forgiving children can be? Did you ever wonder why growing up makes people lose that gift or forget how to use it? It takes much more energy and causes more stress to hold something against a person than it does to forgive and forget. There are of course things that can only be forgiven from afar. If someone repeatedly treats you badly you can forgive them and forget them too.

Self-esteem deficiencies are also an obstacle to giving and receiving love. It is impossible to love someone who doesn't love themselves. It is impossible to be loved if you don't first love yourself. It is possible though, through giving love, to help someone learn to love themselves. I know of a couple who helped each other kick a bad drug habit by first getting help, then supporting and loving each other through the process.

Trying to help someone change and trying to change someone are very different things. Believing that one person can change another can be a trap that two people easily fall into. One person ends up supplying all the love for both people and eventually gets tired of working overtime. Women in particular can make this mistake often.

Trying to change someone looks like devoted, unconditional love on the surface. However, it is really a safe and socially acceptable way of focussing attention on everyone and everything else in order to avoid the more difficult task of looking inside at one's own needs and issues that require attention. Giving in itself is good and healthy. It is a sign of strength. Giving too much or giving without ever receiving something in return, however, means you are giving to the wrong person. I've seen people, often women, who are just like the tree in the children's story about the boy and the giving tree. They end up with nothing left but a stump to lean on. This might be fine for a tree but not so great for a person.

Many people who are searching for their 'true love' become so focused on that, they miss other opportunities to give and receive love. I'm not talking about the chocolate mousse kind of love that makes you weak in the knees, but the plain old rice-pudding kind of love that is all around us. It still counts for something.

Intimacy

Intimacy is about reaching out to a spouse or partner, not with our arms and hands, but with our minds and hearts. It is about accepting them and sharing our lives with them. It is also about exposing ourselves, removing our mask and dismantling the many layers of protection that we use to hide our true selves from others. Revealing our thoughts and feelings is like peeling the outer leaves of an artichoke one by one, until we come to the best part, the tender part, the very heart of the artichoke.

To be intimate is to be vulnerable. It is to say: 'Here I am. This is what I am really like. These are the things that inspire me and these are the things that inspire fear in me. Here are my dreams, hopes and ambitions. Here are my doubts, worries and concerns. Here are my beliefs and values. Here are my weaknesses and faults. Can you accept me for who I am and help to bring out the best in me?'

It takes courage to open up and speak frankly to others. After all, many of us have been damaged by past criticism and have lost faith in others. Once our weaknesses are exposed, we fear rejection, betrayal, ridicule, humiliation and loss of control. Yet, we can regain our trust in others by peeling away the layers a little at a time. In fact, if we were to reveal everything at once, we may overwhelm and frighten others, causing them to distance themselves from us. So, a good rule of thumb is to proceed with baby steps, so that you and your partner slowly and carefully build a solid foundation of mutual trust.

Support builds intimacy. Criticism destroys it. If my partner is slightly overweight, why mention it? Do I think they are so stupid that they don't know they are overweight? And why are they overweight? Perhaps they seek the pleasure of eating to escape the pain of feeling inadequate. So, if I tell them to lose weight, all I do is reinforce their feelings of inadequacy, which leads to more compulsive eating. But if I were to accept them without criticism, this would boost their confidence and perhaps reduce their need to look for pleasure in food. Also, as we grow closer, they may decide to join me at the gym for workouts, which may remove the excess weight and give them even more confidence.

But isn't it true that at times we should speak up? If a close friend or spouse has an addiction that is destroying their life, for example, we should use full force in encouraging them to seek professional help.

Too often, however, we are tempted to ask others to change when we are the ones that need changing. We need to change by growing more accepting of others. Any advice that we offer should be used very sparingly. A useful guideline is: if it is not truthful and not helpful, don't say it; if it is truthful and not helpful, don't say it; if it is not truthful and helpful, don't say it; if it is truthful and helpful, wait for the right time.'

Most people get married believing a myth – that marriage or any relationship is a beautiful box full of all the things they have longed for: companionship, sexual fulfilment, intimacy and friendship. The truth is that marriage, at the start, is an empty box. You must put something in before you can take anything out. There is no love in marriage; love is in people. There is no romance in marriage; people have to infuse it into their marriages. A couple must learn the art and form the habit of giving, loving, serving, praising – keeping the box full. If you take out more than you put in, the box will be empty.

Harsh Talk

Have you been hurt by harsh talk? Most of us have. When verbally assaulted, we recoil and sometimes we counter attack. We perceive the attack as coming from outside ourselves. In truth, however, the attack also comes from within. It comes from the meanings we add to the speaker's words. Someone once said, 'We have met the enemy and he is us!' When we are hurt or upset by other's words, we must look to ourselves as 'self-abusers'. It doesn't feel this way when we are accosted, but take a couple of minutes to understand how self-inflicted pain works in this situation. The ultimate cause of your reaction to other's lack of kindness is you. If you acknowledge this, you just might begin to stop wasting time and energy blaming someone else for your hurt, anger or sadness when they speak cruelly. Then you will be free to figure out how you let someone get to you.

Let us get technical for a moment. When you stop to think about words, you realise that you already know these facts. Words are only written or sound symbols. They are not stones or bricks. As sounds, they simply rattle your eardrum. Our brains process both the sounds and the symbolic aspects of words to give them meaning. It is our interpretation of words that is the true cause of our emotional reactions. In short, your brain and mind act as filters and barriers between incoming words and your reactions to them.

Let me illustrate how it is meaning and not words themselves, that hold power over you. Imagine that someone you love calls you vile names in a foreign language. And, imagine that they do it wilfully, intending to hurt and ridicule. You are not hurt in this situation. The reason is obvious, you do not understand the meaning of the words. Therefore, you cannot attribute hurtful thoughts to the symbols you hear. You may be puzzled or curious, but not hurt.

Notice that you are in control of understanding, not the loud-mouthed or cruel speaker. Even if you get the correct translation and it is truly an insult, the key factor is still the nature of the implications which you attribute to the communication. We assign meaning by a rapid and often pre-conscious thought, such as, 'If she really loved me, she wouldn't talk like that to me'. Then, we react. But, the reaction is caused by our view that there is a threat, for example, the loss of affection. We all know that others can talk harshly and yet not lose long-term affection for us. In short, what they meant was not what we believed they meant!

And this word 'meant' exposes another error we often make in thinking about the power of words to influence us. We think that when the speaker is serious, or really means to hurt us, then the words are even more powerful in their ability to wound. This is not so. The sincerity and strength of a speaker's intention does not guarantee their goal will be accomplished. A New Year's Eve intention is a great example of having a goal which may never be fulfilled. And, what's more, some very strong intentions often have an entirely different impact from that sought. For example, have you ever told a joke with the purpose of amusing someone? Instead of realising your goal, your words might have fallen flat. When a joke fails to amuse, it is because the hearer did not 'get' it; they did not impute the meanings that the teller intended.

The next time you feel criticised or hurt, notice your reaction. Resist the temptation to think 'How dare you!' Ask yourself, 'What do I take that remark to mean?' You may spot an area of personal vulnerability. This is great because this knowledge empowers you to confront and reinforce your areas of weakness.

In summary, words carry meanings and can reveal the speaker's intent. What you do with those meaning is your responsibility. The speaker is solely responsible for his tongue waggling. Learn to use their opinion as an opportunity to inoculate yourself from self-hurt.

Apologising

Because of our imperfections, we occasionally say and do hurtful things. That's why the two very important words in any relationship are 'I apologise'. True, an apology cannot undo the harm already done, but at least it can restore the dignity of the victim. Some are fearful of apologising, believing it to be a sign of weakness. Refusing to apologise is not a sign of strength but weakness. After all, one who refuses to say they're sorry acts out of fear, but one who admits they were wrong and asks for forgiveness acts out of courage.

What do you do if your apology is rejected? Respect the right of the victim to do so. Yet, if your misconduct was not exceptionally grave and your apology was sincere, their refusal to accept it makes them equally guilty, for now they are being hurtful. At such a time, don't perpetuate the problem by expressing anger. Rather, acknowledge that you've arrived at this point because of your own misconduct, accept the humiliation, forgive the person you offended and move on.

Ironically, our misconduct can act as a blessing in disguise, for it is an opportunity to awaken to our faults, express remorse and change our ways by repenting. It is an opportunity for spiritual growth. Remember, however, that this opportunity came about at the expense of another, so don't forget the pain you inflicted and do everything in your power to eliminate it.

More reasons for and benefits of apologising include the following:

- Justice and fairness demand that we apologise any time we hurt others.

- It is an opportunity to grow more spiritual by practising humility.

- It is a gift we offer our victim, for by showing them they are worthy of an apology, we are offering them respect and restoring the esteem we took away by the offence.

- It can heal damaged relationships, for by apologising, we are expressing that the relationship is important to we and we want to make amends.

- When we recognise and accept our weaknesses, we'll be better able to do the same for others, which is important because people are imperfect, mistakes will be made and apologies will have to be accepted to restore harmony.

Apologies play a crucial role in family life. Parents need to treat their children with dignity and apologise when they are wrong. Likewise, children need to treat their parents with respect and say they are sorry when they misbehave. But how can children do so unless they learn from the example of their parents? Parents that are constantly squabbling set a poor example. Husbands and wives must beware of taking their mate for granted. Being married is no excuse for treating your partner unfairly and rudely. On the contrary, no one is more worthy of respect and appreciation than your spouse, so if you occasionally slip up, apologise as quickly as possible and make amends. Apologies and forgiveness, like love and trust, begin with a decision, so make a decision today to never take your spouse or children for granted. If you commit to them, they will commit to you.

An apology isn't complete unless we take all of the following steps.

1. Apologise quickly because we do not know how soon it will be too late.

2. Admit what we did.

3. Express our sorrow.

4. Be sincere by speaking from the heart and feeling the victim's pain.

5. Give our victim the opportunity to vent their feelings.

6. Make up for the harm we've done by taking corrective action, offering compensation or making restitution.

7. Learn from the experience. Mistakes and misbehaviours can prove to be a valuable opportunity to become a better person. Nevertheless, it remains true that the greatest gift we can offer others is to lead a life that doesn't need any apologies. Although it is hardly likely that any of us can reach that ideal, we must cling to it to limit the damage we cause.

Mind the Daddy!

A recent national survey on marital breakdown found that over 70 per cent of couples who attended relationship counselling had children under the age of eleven. In brief, children put pressures on relationships. The first year of parenthood is essential in setting the patterns that will ensure all the family will be happy. Effective parenting can only begin when both the new mother and father feel safe and respected in their new role. So how can we do this? The easiest way is to remember that the happiness of the child is directly linked to the emotional stability of the parents. Both partners have to ensure they protect the psychological space of their husband or wife.

It may be safe to say that fathers experience more surprises after the birth of their baby than their female counterparts. This may be because the reality has already hit the mother long ago. After all, she's been carrying the child for nine months and has been painfully aware of the physical and emotional changes commensurate with having a baby! So what can a new father expect?

Many fathers expect things to get a bit more frantic after the birth of their child, but many do not realise the toll sleep deprivation will take. Concentration, mood and energy levels will be tested to breaking point. However, if both partners work together a good system of rest will develop for both partners.

A new baby can cause fathers to experience an all-consuming love they were never aware was possible. Fatherhood is indeed a daunting responsibility. Right now, you're responsible for the physical well-being of your child. Later on you will serve as the child's role model. While new mothers worry over their ability to nurture, new fathers are often anxious about providing for mother and child.

It is a well-known fact that many women experience post-partum depression. However, men often sink into a case of the baby blues after the birth too! Why? Your partner will be occupied with the new bundle of joy and you may feel left out. You'll also be expected to go back to work relatively quickly and won't get that same new-dad attention you've been feeding off lately. Don't worry, your depression isn't hormonally based, so things should soon return back to 'normal'. And remember, expressing your feelings to your partner will help speed that recovery.

This is no longer about just the two of you. Enter a third variable. Jealousy is an issue for many new fathers. The emotion hits many a man as they observe their partner constantly breastfeeding the newborn. You may start to perceive the baby as something that is coming between you and your partner. Don't bottle up these feelings; let them be known to your significant other. Get alone time with your partner, even if you can only manage a few minutes a day.

Remember, there will be lots of highs and lows, but you'll eventually get into the groove of things. Stay strong.

Honour and Respect

Great numbers of people crave respect. They want to validate their existence. They want to find a reason for living. So they chase after trophies, medals, plaques, awards, prizes and fame. If they win recognition, they can then say, 'Look! I'm special!' They need the recognition of their peers because of low self-esteem. Yet, after receiving congratulations on their achievements, they feel empty inside. They feel like fakes, not worthy of the acclaim. That's because a sense of worthiness can only come from within.

What's the best way to fill the void, satisfy our need for recognition and reclaim our self-esteem? It is by consciously leading an honourable life; by respecting others, by treating them with kindness, generosity and compassion. When we do so, we will recognise our own worth. Also, if we lead virtuous lives, our actions will not go unnoticed. Respect commands itself and it can neither be given nor withheld when it is due.

Although virtue is its own reward and an honourable life will be recognised, our actions should be motivated not by our needs, but by the needs of those we choose to serve. Why do we act honourably? Because life is tough and others need our help. We act with honour not to receive honour, but to fulfil our potential and lead a meaningful life. I'm sure you agree with Plutarch who said, 'We ought not to treat living creatures like shoes or household belongings, which when worn with use we throw away'.

Not everyone can be an astronaut, Taoiseach or a brilliant footballer. However, everyone can be honourable. All human beings are worthy of our respect. Those who are wise realise that it is not what we do, but what we are that counts.

Respect and the Family

Respect begins in the family and is important enough to be a commandment of God: 'Honour thy father and thy mother.' (Exodus 20:12) Why is it so important? Because it is the foundation of a stable society. First peace and harmony in the home, then in the community and finally in the world. Imagine all the problems we could solve if we respected one another. If all boys respected their mothers, would they grow up to be men that abandon the mothers of their children? If we respected our neighbours, regardless of their race, religion or ethnic background, would there be so much bloodshed around the globe? If we respected others, would there be so many break-ins, assaults, rapes and murders?

Where did we go wrong? It all starts at home. Parents are supposed to be role models for their children. They are supposed to teach respect by their example. They are supposed to earn the respect of their children. Yet, instead of being respected, children can be slapped, shouted at, told to shut up, harshly disciplined and treated as prisoners. Children have enough to contend with at school. They have to deal with bullies, thieves, drug pushers, lies, rejection and jeers. Don't you think they need a safe haven, a refuge where they will receive comfort, security, encouragement and love? What a disappointment when they learn that instead of being picked up and embraced, they are dumped on by their own parents! How can they have respect for their parents?

Without receiving respect they cannot learn to give it! Not experiencing respect, they grow up to become cold-hearted adults.

Parents should realise that peace and harmony in the family flow from respect, not from rules, discipline, orders, policy and demands. They need to understand that people are respectable only as they respect. If we have some respect for people as they are, we can be more effective in helping them to become better than they are.

The problem isn't only between parents and children. It is also between husbands and wives. What happened to the vows we made to love, respect and honour each other? Can respect coexist with snide remarks, cold looks, frowns and complaints? Can children respect parents that do not respect each other? Our spouse not only deserves the same respect that any human being is entitled to, but much more. If we are guilty of disrespecting a family member, we need to change our behaviour, remembering that honour isn't only about making the right choices; it's also about taking responsibility for our actions. For the good of mankind, may we all succeed in leading honourable lives.

Appreciation

It costs nothing to compliment your partner and it really feels good to receive compliments. We are often slow about paying compliments to our spouse, letting them know that we think they are pretty, handsome, smart, clever, well-dressed, kind, a good parent etc. We do not have to wait until some occasion when we purchase a greeting card to let our partner know that we think they are special. If we do not compliment each other then who will? It is not just something we should try to do but instead it is an essential behaviour for a successful relationship. Your spouse chose you because when they were with you they felt a positive mirroring of themselves. They felt alive, respected and loved. If this ceases, what is the point in being together? After all, we can find plenty of people to put us down and make us feel bad but very few who can go beneath and compliment us just for being ourselves.

Appreciation is a predisposition, an inclination, openness and readiness of the heart to notice the person who has chosen us and to sense that our chosen relationship is an awesome thing, not to be taken lightly or for granted. An attitude of appreciation colours our perception of our relationship and everything that happens within it. Thanking your partner for making dinner or taking out the rubbish, picking up clothes from the dry-cleaners and in general letting them know that they are appreciated can go a long way towards creating a caring environment. Couples are very quick to criticise one another when tasks do not get done, but they can be very remiss when it comes to showing appreciation. The above two points are based on the psychological process of reciprocation. If human beings are given a gift or shown appreciation it initiates a 'click-whirr' process in the brain. In other words, it creates an automatic response in us. Instead of constantly looking at your partner's negative side, try using the reciprocation rule and watch what happens. One very simple way to use this rule is by doing an 'appreciation letter'.

Doing an Appreciation Letter

Appreciation letters are so simple that it's a wonder that the world isn't overflowing with them. The soft language of approval and gratitude wrapped in a letter that is intimate and special is a powerful way of appreciating your partner. Try writing an appreciation letter to your partner – I guarantee you they will respond and reciprocate your love!

Use these steps:

- Think of a special name, past or present, that only you call your spouse; use this special name in the letter.

- Begin the letter with the simple words: 'I appreciate you because ...'

- Tell your partner the special things you notice about them.

- Using the following words to start sentences tell your partner how empty your life would be without them: 'Without you in my life I would feel ...'

- End the letter by simply saying, 'I love you'.

- Finally, and this is the most important step, place the letter on your partner's pillow or, for even more surprise, post it to them.

Wait and watch what happens. You will be surprised how quickly your partner reciprocates!

Chapter 5

Raising a Happy Child

Listening

Do you have a child living under your roof who seems unwilling or unable to tell you their concerns, worries or even their daily goings-on? Well, join the pack of mothers and fathers who feel that they just can't seem to break into their kids' hearts and heads no matter what they try. And to make the situation even more puzzling, you may even have another child in the same house who babbles constantly about their feelings, what you've done to mess up their life or the details of their friends' daily activities. Sometimes you wish that your budding talk-show host's chatter would rub off on their more reticent sibling!

Well, both styles can be fine, but each comes with pros and cons. You're never quite sure how to react when your talkative one has a meltdown – are they really in a state of crisis or will they recover before dinnertime? But at least they keep you informed of their daily ups and downs so you can keep a finger on their emotional barometer. What about the child who rarely shares their feelings and at times seems to have none, even when you know that their heart has been broken or their pride hurt? That's tough and it takes some savvy parenting to help the reticent communicator to open up.

Setting the Stage

There are some basic dos and don'ts for encouraging your kids to communicate with you. Set the stage for gaining your child's trust in confiding in you as early as possible. Habits begun at a young age are easier to form and have greater staying power. Try not to be critical when your child complains to you about a problem.

If, for example, your initial impulse is to blame your son ('And what did you do to provoke Michael to hit you?'), he'll most likely think twice before sharing his problems with you again in the near future. Making assumptions like this can be off base and damaging to a relationship. Gather the facts before jumping to conclusions. By listening first, you're telling your child that you are on the same team and that you're there for them, although you may not always agree with their thoughts or actions.

To encourage your child to use you as a sounding board or a confidant, you need to have consistent private time with each other. Bedtime lends itself to introspection. It's a time to wrap up the day, both emotionally and physically, and if your evening routine contains this ritual, it becomes second nature to use it as talking time.

Be especially sensitive during times when your child searches you out to talk. Even if your kids have the uncanny knack of uncorking their emotions in the middle of your important phone calls, take the time to listen. I know that it may be inconvenient to break from your thoughts or work in order to pay attention, but if you don't take advantage of the moment, you may not have it again.

Self-esteem

Very often as we trundle our way through life we continually hear the words 'self-esteem'. It is the cornerstone of our being. It influences how we see the world and indeed how we feel we are treated as we journey through life. As parents we know that building our child's sense of self-esteem is important. It is a gift which if we nurture will bring our child through hard times in their life and, more importantly, will set them up to be a positive influence on the future of our society. However, knowing self-esteem is important is not the same as knowing how to give your child a strong sense of self-worth. There is no simple strategy but there are several effective techniques parents can use to help boost self-esteem in their child.

Let them Know their Value

The most important strategy is to show and tell your child how much you value them and appreciate them. Spend time with them, talk to them and really listen to what they have to say and appreciate the things that interest them. If your child gives you the opportunity to enter their world, take it with both hands!

Empower them to Make Decisions

Teach your child about decision making and recognising when they have made a good decision. Children make decisions all the time but often are not aware that they are doing so. There are a number of ways parents can help children improve their ability to consciously make wise decisions. Start first by giving children the ability to make decisions, for example, about what to wear for the day and then letting them live with the consequences, such as being too hot in a long-sleeve shirt or even enduring the cold because they refuse to wear a jumper. Then gradually expand the scope of their decisions and discuss the problems and solutions involved to help the child evaluate the decisions they make.

Make them Responsible for their Emotions

Let children know they create and are responsible for any feeling they experience. Likewise, teach them that they are not responsible for others' feelings. Avoid blaming children for how you feel. Model appropriate ways to respond for their emotions.

Help them Find their Niche

Encourage your child to develop hobbies and interests that give then pleasure and that they can pursue independently. These can help them develop various skills which may help build confidence as well as provide comfort and distraction during difficult times. Also, these may provide common ground to further social interaction with others.

Let them Work it Out with Peers

Children must learn to work out disputes with siblings, friends and classmates without adult intervention. As they grow older they won't always be under direct adult supervision; furthermore learning to work through social challenges can help build confidence and self-esteem. Another important social tool is the ability to cope with teasing. Help your child develop 'tease tolerance' by pointing out that some teasing can't hurt and exploring the reasons why some kids tease.

Show them their Strengths

When your child succeeds at something, reinforce that success by pointing out how far they have come by not giving up. When your child fails, point out the other successes they have enjoyed, especially those that were accomplished after a failure.

Teach them to Laugh

Laugh with your children and encourage them to laugh at themselves. People who take themselves very seriously are undoubtedly decreasing their enjoyment in life. A good sense of humour and the ability to make light of life are important ingredients for increasing one's overall enjoyment. Laughter is a great stress reliever and a good way to make friends. Laughing at your mistakes and at life's challenges help teach children to put trouble in perspective and cope with challenges.

Using these seven strategies can help build your child's self-esteem and help them lead a happier and more successful life.

Limits

What do you tell your children when they say they need expensive shoes so they can be 'popular' at school? If their shoes cost more than yours, isn't something wrong? Children are afraid they won't be 'loved' by their peers if they wear cheap clothes, and parents can be afraid they won't be 'loved' by their children if they don't give in to their demands. I don't mean to imply that expensive shoes are inherently bad. Not at all. If your child has a part-time job and buys their own shoes, they are learning valuable lessons. For example, they are learning that hard work is rewarded and that they can set goals and reach them – not to mention self-reliance.

No, there's nothing wrong with expensive shoes, but there is something wrong with the belief that one is entitled to receive them. Your kids are entitled to shoes, but not to choosing the brand, unless all brands cost the same. Parents may give in to their children's demands because of guilt, especially if both parents work and they don't spend as much time with their children as they would like to. They may comply because they are afraid their children won't like them if they refuse or simply to end their children's nagging. None of these are the right reasons for acting and they all teach our children terrible lessons.

When we give in because of guilt or convenience, we teach our children how to manipulate us. Girls who pick up this skill can grow up to manipulate young men into spending money on gifts. Such women develop shaky relationships that are bound to crumble and lead to unhappiness. Boys can grow up into men that try to manipulate others in the workplace, a practice that can only lead to long-term problems.

Instead of giving in to peer pressure, our children should be given the opportunity to develop courage, responsibility and individualism. Rather than blindly following the whims of others, why not set the trends? Of course, some conforming to social pressure is both acceptable and desirable. We have to learn how to conform to the laws of the land and the rules of the workplace, but our will must never be handed over blindly. Conformity must be preceded by careful thought. We should willingly and happily conform to whatever helps us and society. However, we should resist and peacefully try to change any rules, customs or habits that would harm ourselves or others. Give your children the support and courage to be themselves. If someone makes fun of them, let them remember to say, 'I'm not in this world to live up to your expectations and you're not in this world to live up to mine'.

To resist peer pressure, kids need to have sufficient self-esteem. They have to recognise and appreciate their own value. But how can they do so if they are constantly criticised at home? Often the little praise they do receive is quickly replaced by expectations. For example, parents urge their children to excel at school and when they do so, they are praised at first. However, as they continue to do well in school, the parents expect this behaviour, stop praising them and miss no opportunity to criticise them. If children's needs for recognition and belonging are not fulfilled at home, is it surprising that they look for it among their peers?

When we tell our children it is okay to buy expensive shoes to be popular at school, we are teaching them to be shallow. We are teaching them to judge people by what they wear or have instead of by what they are. Shallow young men search for a pretty face and an attractive figure. Shallow young women search for men with a good car and a decent job. What happened to values such as faithfulness, integrity, devotion, understanding, patience, encouragement and unconditional love? When the foundation for marriage becomes a pretty face and a nice car, why are we surprised by the number of divorces?

For their own good and the good of others, don't let your children play with fire. Teach them responsibility. Our job is to prepare our children for life by teaching them values. When we fail to prepare them, we are clipping their wings and hampering their future growth. They need to learn that we develop our potential by contributing to society, not by getting a free ride.

We did not decide to make the sky blue, grass green or summers warm, but that doesn't mean we can't appreciate them. True, your children didn't choose their parents, their place of birth or their circumstances, but that doesn't mean they can't appreciate them. Unless we learn how to be grateful for what we have, how will we appreciate what we will have in the future? We need to own less, not more. The more we own, the less we appreciate what we have. If we want our children to be happy, we need to help them understand this.

Isn't it odd how something as insignificant as the shoes we wear can have such an impact on our lives? Perhaps we need to look a little more closely at the decisions we make.

The In-Charge Parent

For many of us the natural tendency is to indulge our children – we all want them to have a great childhood and have treasured memories of that childhood. And of course it is important that children do get special gifts and have treats, but remember what makes these treats all the more special is the fact that they do not happen every day.

It sounds strange but while happiness is a desirable emotional state, compassion and empathy are developed through feeling sorrow and pain. Many parents today seem afraid to have their children feel and express any feeling but happy. We are not talking about concern for a child that is showing signs of depression; rather, parental anxiety about a child experiencing the normal ups and downs of childhood.

Complicating this fear is the phenomenon of some parents inviting their children to like them and treat them as if they were best friends. There are parents who are afraid to say 'No' to their children and even bribe compliance or a smile with treats. Children need to know who heads the family, who cares enough to protect, set limits and has a sense of firm leadership.

Please note there are some parents who would benefit from minimising some of their 'No's' and replacing a few of them with 'Yes'. A simple tip is to remember the Grandmother Rule or 'After' Rule: 'Yes, after your homework is done you may play.'

Instead of having children who always feel happy, don't we want children who will shed a tear at their grandparent's funeral, who will feel angry with bullying behaviour and afraid for the toddler who waddles into traffic? Let's agree that all feelings are valid and we want to aim for children who will become healthy and contributing citizens who choose kind and responsible behaviours.

If we start with that premise, we will see the role of parent embracing functions of a teacher, guider, counsellor, encourager and nurturer rather than a fairy or magic genie that can create happy miracles and lives on another planet. Clearly established rules, guidelines and family values are modelled and led by parents who want children living with balanced emotions.

Parents need to become the authority figures of their family. The parenting practice of giving choices for all manner of daily behaviour can backfire. Parents need to balance their managing choices (with consequences) with training for compliance and teaching life skills. As children mature there are personal aspects that we want them to be thoughtfully choosing. Yet, we want all citizens compliant to the rules of society. Just as you and I stop habitually at the red stop signs, children can be taught to respond consistently to routines and household rules – assuming they are age appropriate and fair.

Establishing rules, directing, teaching, correcting and insisting are all qualities of the in-charge parent. The following are some tips that may help:

- Work from more structure to less structure, not the other way around.

- Rules worth having are worth enforcing.

- Whenever possible, discipline should end with the correct behaviour, not with a punishment.

- Limit children to the choices that are theirs to make.

- If adults won't say 'No' to children, children won't say 'No' to themselves.

Deciding that all feelings are acceptable and that you are primarily responsible for providing loving care, guidance and structure will free you to say 'No' and 'Yes' when necessary and appropriate. If you find the going tough, just remember – the happiest children in the playground are not the ones who are used to always getting their own way.

Child Teachers

'Children today are tyrants. They contradict their parents, gobble their food and tyrannise their teachers.' Sound familiar? Who do you suppose said that? It was Socrates! He said that more than 2,400 years ago. So the world hasn't changed much, has it? It seems middle-aged people feel threatened by youngsters. They don't like their 'rude' behaviour and the way they dress. What has changed, however, is not the behaviour of children, but our own memory. We forget what it's like to be a child.

There are few places outside their own play where a child can contribute to the world in which they live. Their world is dominated by adults who tell them what to do and when to do it – benevolent tyrants who dispense gifts to their 'good' subjects and punishment to their 'bad' ones, who are amused at the 'cleverness' of children and annoyed by their 'stupidities'.

True, there is youth crime and violence, but perhaps this is a case of children doing to society what was done to them. Where do you suppose most abandoned children live? At home! Though they live at home, many children are ignored by their parents. Perhaps kids run away from home because they're looking for their parents. When children are deprived of love, why are we surprised that they turn out bad? There's something wrong when the TV set is better adjusted than our kids, but whose fault is that? The truth is children are a godsend. We can learn from them. That's why Christ said, 'Truly, I say to you, unless you turn and become like children, you will never enter the kingdom of heaven' (Matthew 18:3).

Children are pure. They are innocent. See how they play with their neighbours. Race, ethnicity, religion and gender are foreign to them. Everyone is valued as a friend and all are treated equally (until adults interfere and teach them prejudice).

Children are honest. They speak from their hearts. Adults wear masks, hiding their thoughts. They are afraid to speak the truth, afraid to expose their true selves. Not so for children, for they have courage. John Bradshaw explains: 'Children are curious and are risk-takers. They have lots of courage. They venture out into a world that is immense and dangerous. A child initially trusts life and the processes of life.'

Children can make us more spiritual. They are bubbling over with happiness and unconditional love. To become like children is to love the world unconditionally. We create children, but they create spiritual beings by teaching us the power of love. Also, learn from children the joy of simple pleasures. To a three-year-old child, a green caterpillar can be more exciting than a €300 see-saw.

Our primary responsibility to children is to guard their happiness and return their love. They don't need our presents; they need our presence. Mark Twain explains: 'We are always too busy for our children; we never give them the time or interest they deserve. We lavish gifts upon them; but the most precious gift – our personal association, which means so much to them – we give grudgingly.'

How can children learn how to live right if they've never seen it done? They need models, not critics. They will follow our example, not our advice. So, how shall we teach them? By example!

Parents are often heard to say, 'Pay attention when I speak'. But why don't we pay attention when children speak? The smallest event in your child's life is an event in their world. It is, therefore, a world event. To your child it is significant; pay attention to it.

Your children are in critical need of nurturing. They need your encouragement, praise and support. They need a willing ear to hear their concerns and a tight hug that expresses your unconditional acceptance and total commitment. Don't worry about what they will be tomorrow, but focus on what they are today. The best way to bring up children is never to let them down. Here's a tip that comes from Lady Bird Johnson: 'Believe in them; children are apt to live up to what you believe of them.'

We also need to teach our children responsibility. As Ann Landers wrote: 'What the vast majority of children needs is to stop being pampered, stop being indulged, stop being chauffeured, stop being catered to. In the final analysis it is not what you do for your children but what you have taught them to do for themselves that will make them successful human beings.'

When you were a youngster, your mother quickly mended your torn jacket. But when the harsh words of your parents bruised your heart, how many years did it take for your heart to heal? Perhaps it still hurts. Your parents meant well. They didn't know better, so forgive them. Learn from their mistakes and avoid bruising the hearts of your children.

Tenderness

It doesn't take a rocket scientist to understand that receiving loving attention in childhood leads to better emotional health in adulthood. In a recent study of 2,905 women and men aged 25 to 74, researchers at the State University of New York at Albany School of Public Health found that it can help adults beat the odds of getting any number of diseases, too.

The study found that people who said their parents were nurturing had fewer incidences of many chronic physical conditions, including diabetes, high blood pressure and arthritis. In contrast, those who gave their parents low marks on such questions as 'How much did your mother understand your problems and worries?' or 'How much time and attention did your father give to you when you needed it?' reported more illness.

'People who receive strong support from their parents develop stronger coping mechanisms that help them deal with challenges in healthy ways,' says study author Benjamin Shaw, PhD, a behavioural psychologist.

How can you learn to stay emotionally connected as your child grows? It boils down to being there and being willing to listen. Here are some age-by-age strategies.

Pre-school
Strategy: Mix togetherness with time for your children to explore on their own. The push for independence vies with the need for security; requests to soothe a bumped head or admire a cool caterpillar can be bids for reassurance. Show that you're a participant in their lives physically and emotionally.

Primary school
Strategy: Show that you care, even if your child says it's uncool. Even though kids at this age outwardly push their parents away, they want their support and approval. Those who feel that their parents care are better protected from most primary school health risks and behavioural problems. So schedule fun time together – it's a great way to show that you care and that you're available.

Secondary school

Strategy: Skip the tirade about alcohol, drugs and sex – stick with the facts. They need honesty. If they think it's a rant, they tune parents out. Instead, talk with your teen realistically. Set ground rules and discuss safe ways to avoid potential dangers, such as calling home for a lift instead of getting into a car with a drunk driver. The candid approach can build deeper trust.

Responsible Children

We would all like our children to develop into responsible people. How can we help to ensure that our kids learn the lessons of responsibility? Here are some ideas:

Start them with tasks when they're young

Young kids have a strong desire to help out, even as young as the age of two. They can do a lot more than you think if you're patient and creative. This helps build confidence and enthusiasm for later tasks in their life.

Don't use rewards with your kids

If you want your kids to develop an intrinsic sense of responsibility, they need to learn the 'big picture' value of the things they do. They won't learn that if they're focused on what they're going to 'get'.

Use natural consequences when they make mistakes

If they keep losing their football gloves somewhere, let them deal with the consequences. Maybe they will have to ask to borrow some for the game; maybe they will have to buy new ones if they're lost. If you rescue them every time, they'll never learn responsibility.

Let them know when you see them being responsible
Specifically point out what you like about their behaviour. This will make them more likely to repeat it.

Talk often about responsibility with your kids
Make responsibility a family value; let them know it's important.

Model responsible behaviour for your kids
This is where they'll learn it from. Take care of your stuff. Try to be on time. They're watching you very closely.

Give them an allowance early in their life
Let them make their own money decisions from an early age. They'll learn their lessons in a hurry. Don't bail them out if they run out of money.

Have a strong, unfailing belief that your kids are responsible
They'll pick up on this belief and they'll tend to rise to the level of expectation. Keep believing this even when they mess up!

Train them to be responsible
Use role play and talk to them about exactly what kind of behaviour you expect from them. It's hard for kids to be responsible when they don't know what it really means.

Get some help and support for your parenting
It's hard to know sometimes whether you're being too controlling or too permissive as a parent. Talk to other parents, read books, join parent support groups – whatever will help you feel like you're not alone.

Chapter 6

Work–Life Balance

The Treadmill

You've heard it before: There is more to life than work. You've thought about it and agree that it's a good idea. Perhaps you've even struggled with just how to make that idea a reality in your life. You just can't seem to find that balance between your work and personal life. A recent report entitled 'Off the Treadmill' indicates that Irish people are working longer hours and there are an increasing proportion of households with both partners out at work. In the UK, research on 30,000 workers conducted by academics at the University of Warwick found mental distress and psychological illness had increased significantly.

There are a number of factors that indicate whether you need to address your work–life balance. If work leaves you physically and emotionally drained and you feel like you are accomplishing less and doing more; if you've lost your sense of humour and playfulness and you find yourself short-tempered and angry; finally if you go on holiday but the feeling of being overwhelmed comes back immediately upon return then it is time to take action.

Finding and maintaining a comfortable balance in life is a universal challenge. However, like many psychological dilemmas the first point of control is yourself. Part of the confusion about 'balance' comes from thinking that balance means equal amounts of time. Consider a new definition of balance – paying attention to every aspect of your life on a regular basis. Balance is about living in sync with yourself so you can live with others. It's about attending to your multidimensional self so you can make conscious choices about how you spend your time and energy at work and in life.

There are five aspects of living that need your attention. They are the physical, mental, social, emotional and spiritual dimensions. Too little attention to any one of them will create the feeling of being out of sync with your self. Appropriate attention to each dimension will give you the power to find the right mix of priorities and actions for creating a balance between life and work. When you're in balance, you are more creative, more productive and can truly experience the process of life.

Here are some actions you can take in each of the dimensions that will assist you in creating more balance between work and life:

- Reflect about your personal goals and behaviour. Take time for yourself on a daily basis. Meditate, commune with nature or read inspirational material. Get a massage. Sit and do nothing. Become comfortable with who you are outside of your title and occupation.

- Look for ways to eliminate time-bandits by saying 'No' to requests that don't fit with your master plan. Let go of perfectionist tendencies about how things should be. Set goals that allow you to discover yourself and pursue a variety of interests unrelated to work.

- Nurture your relationships. Never cancel on your kids or partner. Do things for their pure enjoyment. Laugh often, especially at the silly things you do. Look for the humour in life.

- At the end of the work day, release all your concerns so you can be ready for time outside of work. Leave work at work. Creating and maintaining balance in life is worth the effort right now because you'll live a richer life, enjoy the process of living and nurture your relationships while being true to your own essence.

The Clock

Is there any stress in your life that doesn't involve time, with deadlines, business meetings, shopping, school events and doctor's appointments? Most people today are time starved. Instead of being a valuable resource, time becomes a toxic enemy. It's the wall you keep bumping up against. Those well-intentioned, self-care to-do items never get done. You end up feeling out of control. Worse, toxic time leads to chronic stress, which harms your health.

Want to turn this around? First, don't wait until everything's under control before resolving the problem. That'll never happen. Instead, take command of your time today. Grab your calendar and make the changes that will bring you peaceful enjoyment.

Stop Being a Prisoner of the Clock!

Follow these two simple techniques to make better use of the hours in your day.

1. Be prepared for toxic time withdrawal. Don't expect overnight changes. Instead, gently apply the brakes to your speedy life, then be patient. You'll initially feel uncomfortable adjusting to the unfamiliar slower pace of living. That's because you may actually be addicted to the speed of your current life. You need time to withdraw from the toxic frenzy.

2. Force yourself to do something s-l-o-w-l-y. Making a pot of soup is ideal. Enjoy every slow minute of vegetable chopping, broth boiling and seasoning. Sit down (no standing allowed!) and take time to thoroughly enjoy the savoury concoction.

Make a time inventory

Is your calendar full of overlapping commitments? Try this: study a calendar and list everything – commuting, errands, working, time with friends, housework, sleeping and so on. Calculate how much time you spend in each category. If you see a category where you spend too much time then do something about it! Fill some of the rescued time with self-care activities (exercise, reading, shopping etc.). Ink them in and don't eliminate them first when there's a time crunch.

Treat time like money

You don't throw your money away, yet you give your time away as though it were free. Learn how to prioritise. Make those hard decisions about how you want to spend your time. Tell yourself, I won't add another thing to my schedule. If I want to do this, I'll have to give up something else. Don't spend time that you don't have!

Here's a little tip: the next time you're waiting for something (traffic jam, shopping queue, on hold on the phone), realise that it's a golden opportunity to grab some peace. Sit back, let your mind go and, if you can, close your eyes and take several deep breaths. You have now converted a few minutes of frustration into a rejuvenating break.

Schedule time for joy

List the things that you find joyful. Getting out to the park for a walk, writing in your journal, doing knitting (trust me it's good for you!), reading a novel or window-shopping all qualify. You can plan these events or you can make them happen when you have downtime. Carry your journal (or knitting, or novel) with you and keep your walking shoes in your car.

When your client cancels a meeting or an appointment gets rescheduled, instead of filling the time with more work, how about a compromise? Spend thirty minutes working and thirty minutes doing a joyful activity.

That Man Thing!

Here are some disturbing realities for men in today's world:

- Men are only half as likely as women to live to age 85.
- Men die earlier than women from all fifteen of the leading causes of death.
- Men make more money but have a lower net worth than women.
- The frequency of suicide in males is increasing while decreasing for females.
- No government agency spends as much on men's health as on women's health.

What does this mean? Stress and the demand to perform at ever higher levels of achievement are killing men and reducing their quality of life. Here are five things men can do to increase their chances of living a full life:

1. **Drop the facade of strength at all costs.** The need to appear 'strong' may be the primary cause of untimely death. Talk with women. Talk with other men. Talk with your doctor, counsellor, priest or

friend. Be willing to say 'I don't know', 'I'm afraid', 'I feel …' or 'I can't …'. The idea that you must be strong 'at all costs' may be killing you. Let go of the idea you have to be strong for everyone else; it's your life you'll be saving.

2. **Be willing to make lasting changes.** Men tend to find temporary outlets or relief for stress. They suppress it, have an affair, take a second job, start a new sport, begin more exercise, go to another seminar, smoke more cigarettes, eat more fatty foods or drink more beer. The net effect of coping in these ways is an increased incidence of cancer, heart disease and other stress-related diseases.

3. **Examine all of your options.** Generally, men see only two options in life: work full-time or die. This lack of options becomes an obligation. Obligations breed resentment. Most of us suppress, internalise or look for temporary relief from the resentments we feel in our life. None of these are long-term solutions. Use personal writing or journaling to explore your feelings and options. Then, find someone to talk to. If it doesn't feel safe to talk with your spouse, boss, business associates or friends, talk with your physician, priest or a counsellor. Look at all your options. It will give you the real power of choice in your life.

4. **Lose control.** External success and personal responsibility have been the universal measures for men in our society. Always being strong, self-reliant, successful and all-knowing may have been necessary for survival in another place and time, but not now. Losing control can mean seeing new options for your life.

5. **Keep physically fit.** If you aren't taking care of yourself physically – and most men aren't – begin today to change one thing towards living a healthful lifestyle. A ten-minute walk every day may be the only thing between you and a heart attack or depression. See a doctor if you haven't seen one in over a year. If they suggest changes in your lifestyle, make them. Eat healthfully. Get enough sleep. Exercise in moderation. Don't let yourself be lulled into a false sense of security by thinking 'Everything must be in order because I haven't had a heart attack yet'. The body has an extremely high tolerance for stress and many of our temporary relief methods work to hide its symptoms. Tension headaches, dry mouth, pounding pulse, neck and back pain, free-floating anxiety, hives, indigestion, irritability and fatigue are all indicators of stress. Take action before your body says 'I've had all I can take' and quits for good.

Stress

You know your job is stressful and you know in the long run that this is not good for your health. But you don't know what to do about it, or how to change the stressful elements.

It used to be acceptable years ago for the big boss to yell at their subordinates all day, every day. Employees from all different walks of life, vocations, races and geographical locations would have to put up with the stress of the workplace and then go home to their family.

History has shown that people will find a way to decompress – but unfortunately many people never learned healthy ways to do it and their marriages, families etc. suffered because of it. Think of the overworked mother who comes home and releases all her stress by yelling at her children about homework, their friends, their behaviour etc. That creates a different type of stress within the family structure that will be a legacy for those children and their children.

Many people think they don't have time to decompress in 'healthy' ways or ways that they would prefer, so they have an after work drink or smoke. Unfortunately, there are serious health consequences for these types of decompression tactics and they can snowball into crutches and/or addictions.

So what do we do?

1. Some people have to do something before they hit the front door: walk around the block; drive around the block; stop by the supermarket or shopping centre for a few last-minute items.

2. Some people choose to create a bit more time for themselves before coming home and fit in going to the gym for thirty minutes or enrolling in a creative type of class such as paining, ceramics, knitting or going by the library/book shop for a book signing or reading.

3. Other people absolutely have no time between getting off work and getting home or picking up their kids from after-care etc., so the plan needs to happen in the car or when they get home. Make sure you have some of your favourite CDs in the car or an audio book. There is no mandate that you have to start homework or dinner immediately after you hit the door. Take some time to unwind with a magazine or book you've been dying to read. Play a game or dance for thirty minutes with your kids.

4. Finally, there are always the old stand-by's. Try deep breathing and other meditative methods before you move onto another task.

5. Talk about your job with others that will listen. Vent your frustrations and come up with realistic and creative solutions to make your life at the job more manageable.

6. Good employers may offer employee assistance programs, where a person can seek help in coping with stress. Other companies may offer health and wellness programs. Take advantage of them!

Whatever you do, choose something. If you go to work day after day screaming at your peers or your family, or if you are at the receiving end of this behaviour, you have to do something before you deal with the rest of your life. If not you can become a prisoner of the clock and a negative force in your work, home and to yourself.

Time

The price we pay for our endless flurry of activity is high. We are stressed out, burned out and wiped out. Instead of a life of serenity, we lead lives of frustration, resentment and anger. Because we are too busy to have time for anything important, we feel empty. We feel as though we are plodding through a meaningless existence.

We worry about losing time, but not about losing our potential. We work hard for the growth of the company, but ignore our own self-growth. The toll of busyness is also the loss of excellence, for we abandon the practice of doing few things well for that of doing many things poorly. The speed at which we work causes errors and drains our energy that is needed to cope with problems.

How do we fight against the assassination of our spirit? By taking time and making time to collect our thoughts. If we are to move from impulsive action to directed action, we need to take the time to plan, marshal our resources and build our enthusiasm. If we are to go from 'I'm busy' to 'I'm productive', we must make the time to focus on what is important and then take purposeful action.

Our spirit is a creative force that has the power to bring about our dreams. But it needs quiet time to study our options, analyse obstacles and build a road map to success. If we allow ourselves to get ensnared in a cyclone of busyness, the ember of our spirit's dream will be blown out. Many people are too busy worrying about what they've done to think about what they're doing. We have to reverse that trend by being aware of our actions, always thinking before we act, always reflecting on the results of our actions.

The question facing us is: how do we find the time to live? How do we disentangle ourselves from the web of busyness? Traditional approaches have been to turn to time management with the hope of learning how to squeeze extra hours out of the day. Assuming that I uncover another three hours a day to work with, how does that help me if I'm too exhausted to do anything else? So, the solution seems to lie in *energy* management, not *time* management.

One of the best ways to save time is to do things right the first time. 'Desire to have things done quickly prevents their being done properly.' If you agree with that, you agree with the words of Confucius, who taught that in the 6th century BCE. There's something else you can do to regain control of your life and it's something Confucius never thought of: turning off the TV.

Staying up late at night to 'relax' or get extra work done is self-defeating because you are denying your body the rest it needs to perform at top efficiency. Another mistake some make is refusing to say NO to the excessive expectations of family, friends and co-workers. Sure, doing favours is fine, but when others do far less for you than you do for them, it places an unfair burden on you. You keep their friendship, but become your own enemy.

An excellent way to create more time is to perform several goals simultaneously. For example, when you take the family to the park for a game of volleyball, you are enjoying family time, calming the mind with recreation (re-creation), caring for your body with exercise and recharging your spirit with the beauty of nature.

Another factor to consider is your interpretation of 'success'. Are you striving to *have* more or *be* more? I know a lawyer who sold his practice, moved to the country with his family and opened an inn. He and his family have discovered they are getting far more from life, despite their lower income. Do you really need a Hummer or will a Honda Civic do? The savings in the price of the car, insurance, maintenance and gas means you don't have to work as hard. Is it a Hummer you want or happiness? Remember, even if you win the rat race, you remain a rat, trapped in the maze of busyness.

Both busyness and laziness lead to the same end, the neglect of important goals. Our task, then, is to treat time with the respect it deserves. After all, it is both a limited and a non-renewable resource. Time is our lifeblood; it is destined to reap great benefits if we use it wisely. Of course, we cannot change overnight, making a 180-degree turn from a life of busyness to one of purposeful and carefully thought-out action. But we can begin to take baby steps today and bit by bit regain control of our lives.

How can we complain that we don't have enough time when every hour of our lives contains sixty minutes? It's not time that we lack, but the willingness to make tough choices. There comes a time in life when we have to make a choice. And there are only two things to choose. Get busy living or get busy dying. Which one will it be for you?

Balance

Did you ever feel like a tightrope walker trying to keep your balance as you follow your life path? Pope John Paul II describes the feeling: 'Man always travels along precipices. His truest obligation is to keep his balance.' You see, we take on many roles in life, each of which allows us to express a different dimension of our being. It is these separate roles that need to be balanced. Here are some examples. If you are doing well in your career, but your family is complaining that you're not spending enough time with them, your life needs balancing. If it is not only your career, but also your body size that is ballooning, your lifestyle needs balancing. Finally, if you get to prove your skill in yoga, bridge or golf every night, but have no time to fix the leaky tap, mow the lawn or clean the garage – your life needs balancing.

There are two main ways to balance life. Since life coexists with time, the first way to balance life is to balance time. The second way to balance life is by balancing our attitude, perspective or worldview. And we do that by avoiding extremes and taking the middle path. For instance, extreme political views, whether to the right or left, are divisive, but moderate or centrist views are unifying.

We move ahead in life by setting goals and we live a balanced life by setting goals for all our roles. Let's start by looking at our major roles in life and follow that by steps we can take to get better balance.

Career: provides us with the opportunity to earn income, express our personality and develop our potential.

Family: provides us with the chance to express love, assume and share responsibility and contribute to society.

Spirituality: an opportunity to tap into a power greater than ourselves and a source of inspiration. An appreciation of morality, the arts, wonder, awe and nature will heighten our awareness of the spiritual dimension.

Friends: an opportunity to practise sharing and caring, as well as baring our soul.

Solitude: quiet time to recharge our batteries, meditate and make plans. A time to work on improving our emotional and intellectual development. A time set aside to work on self-improvement.

Financial: here's where we plan for the purchase of a car, home ownership, family holidays and a retirement income.

Leisure: fun and recreation release stress and provide opportunities to socialise and develop new skills.

Health: an important component of mind, body and spirit balance. Exercise, a proper diet and sufficient sleep are the ingredients to success in this area.

Now, for some steps you can take to increase the balance in your life.

1. List your various roles and show by percentage how successful you think you are in fulfilling that role. For example, **Career**, 80 per cent; **Family**, 60 per cent; **Health**, 40 per cent and so on. Bringing the present state of imbalance into your awareness is the first step in changing the situation for the better. The areas with the lowest percentage are the areas that need the most work. The areas with the highest percentage show where you are devoting most of your time.

2. Decide how you can divert time from high percentage areas to low percentage areas. As an example, you may want to divert time from your **Career** to your **Family**. You can do this by eliminating wasted time, developing your time (life) management skills, working more efficiently and wresting control of your job rather than letting it control you.

3. Whenever possible, perform several roles at once. For example, if your family joins friends for a volleyball game at the park, you can fulfil several roles at once: **Leisure, Family, Friends, Health** (exercise) and **Spirituality** (by getting in touch with nature and enjoying a sunset in the park). Moreover, if your friend is from work, you would also develop your **Career** role as well.

4. Take control of your life by making deliberate choices. Carefully weigh the costs of living with imbalance. Take corrective action where necessary and regularly monitor and fine-tune your progress.

5. Remember, we are all unique. It is unreasonable to expect everyone to perfectly balance each role in life. After all, part of our uniqueness lies in how we interpret what roles are the most important to us. Great artists, for example, may be consumed by their craft, spending little time elsewhere. Yes, their lives are imbalanced, but of great value to society. So, the important lesson is not about balancing our lives perfectly, but about balancing them in a manner that best expresses our potential and role on earth.

6. Follow the simple laws of *be, do* and *have*. You've got to *be* self-disciplined to *do* the necessary steps to balance your life. And when you do so, you will *have* balance, peace and contentment.

How do you know when your life is balanced? If you can die today, contented with your life, it is balanced!

Insight

Many of us are blind to the joys of life. The cure for this blindness is not sight, but insight. We don't need eyes; we just need understanding. We need understanding of life principles, such as *nothing is what it seems to be*. In other words, something that appears to be 'good' may actually be 'bad', or something that appears to be 'bad' may be 'good'.

Our perspective, perception, viewpoint or attitude should not be based on the input of sensory data; that is, it should not be based on the *appearances* of things. Rather, our view of life should be based on the light of knowledge and understanding. Let's move from the theoretical to the practical. Consider this: judging people is like driving a car – we clearly see the headlights or glaring faults of others, yet our own headlights and faults are invisible to us. When we apply this knowledge, we will stop being offended by the actions (appearances) of others. We will see them not with our eyes, but with our hearts.

I encounter many people complaining that they are not appreciated at work. Can you see the irony in this? The fact that they are complaining about their workplace proves that they do not appreciate their job. Aren't they guilty of the very thing they accuse their employer of? We need to learn that happiness flows not from a particular position, but from a particular disposition. When we maintain the proper disposition, perception or perspective, we enjoy heaven on earth, for heaven is not a matter of altitude, but of attitude. Adopting the correct view of life is essential. It is the difference between happiness and misery, health and sickness and success and failure. Because of its importance, let's consider the following points:

1. Become aware of your perception of life. Are you always cheerful, grateful to be alive? If not, stop complaining because it's unproductive. Rather, understand that perception comes not from what you see, but from what you are. If you are unhappy, the problem lies with you. It is not the world that is unhappy, but *you* that are unhappy, so it is not the world that needs to change, but *you* that needs to.

2. How do you need to change? Begin by realising that there are an infinite number of ways to interpret events. And you have the power to *choose* one of the unlimited viewpoints. You could, for example, choose to look at a particular situation negatively. But why would you want to do that? For such a viewpoint is

harmful. Decide now to stop reacting to life's challenges with automatic responses. Learn to stop and think before you act. See the world with the light of reason and don't judge it by its appearances.

3. Realise that when you choose to see the world differently, you will feel differently. And when you feel differently, you will act differently. Your outlook affects your outcomes, so choose wisely.
6. Deciding to change is not enough. Don't stop with good intentions, but end with good follow-through. Make a plan and complete what you begin.

7. Developing new habits always involves some effort, but don't be discouraged by a little discomfort. Remember, life is not meant to be comfortable; it is meant to be exhilarating.

8. When facing difficulties, remember that they did not come about by dumb luck or blind fate. Luck is not dumb and fate is not blind. It is *you* that are blind. After all, how can you see today how things will turn out tomorrow? Be like the poor farmer and say, with peace of mind, 'That's life'.